Soviet Society Under Gorbachev

Soviet Society Under Gorbachev

Current Trends and the Prospects for Reform

**MAURICE FRIEDBERG and
HEYWARD ISHAM, editors**

M. E. SHARPE, INC.
ARMONK, NEW YORK
LONDON, ENGLAND

Library of Congress Cataloging-in-Publication Data

Soviet society under Gorbachev.

   Papers from a conference on Soviet society convened by the Department
of State and held at Airlie House, Virginia in the fall of 1986.
   Bibliography: p.
   Includes index.
   Contents: The family in the Soviet Union / Mark G. Field — Labor
problems and the prospects for accelerated economic growth / Vladimir
Kontorovich — A noble experiment? / Vladimir Treml — [etc.]
   1. Soviet Union—Social conditions—1970-   —Congresses.
2. Soviet Union—Politics and government—1982-   —Congresses.
I. Friedberg, Maurice, 1929-
II. Isham, Heyward.
HN523.5.S685   1987   947.085′3   87-16572
ISBN 0-87332-442-0
ISBN 0-87332-443-9 (pbk.)

Printed in the United States of America

CONTENTS

Introduction / *Maurice Friedberg*   vii

THE CONTEMPORARY SOVIET FAMILY: PROBLEMS,
ISSUES, PERSPECTIVES / *Mark G. Field*   3

LABOR PROBLEMS AND THE PROSPECTS FOR ACCELERATED
ECONOMIC GROWTH / *Vladimir Kontorovich*   30

A NOBLE EXPERIMENT? GORBACHEV'S
ANTIDRINKING CAMPAIGN / *Vladimir G. Treml*   52

GORBACHEV AND THE SOVIET NATIONALITY
PROBLEM / *Paul A. Goble*   76

GLASNOST' AND SOVIET CULTURE / *Anthony Olcott*   101

MAKING THE MEDIA WORK: SOVIET SOCIETY AND
COMMUNICATIONS / *Ellen Mickiewicz*   131

Afterword / *Heyward Isham*   151

Index   155

INTRODUCTION

Maurice Friedberg

Not since Nikita S. Khrushchev's advent to power over thirty years ago has a change in Soviet leadership given rise to as many great expectations as has Mikhail S. Gorbachev's accession to the helm of state. To be sure, there are parallels that suggest themselves at once. Both men succeeded the two longest-ruling leaders in Soviet history, and both promptly promised rather radical changes, if not a clear break with the past. True, the moderately repressive two decades of Brezhnev's reign (and the brief tenures of Andropov and Chernenko) lack the drama of Stalin's terror-filled era, and Gorbachev, however charismatic, lacks the flamboyancy of Khrushchev. Even had he been so inclined, Gorbachev could not produce a denunciation of his predecessor's bloody crimes that could remotely rival Khrushchev's stirring oration at the 1956 Communist Party Congress. Whatever the differences imposed by history and individual leadership styles (Brezhnev did not lead the nation during the travail of a world war, and he lacked Stalin's tyrannical instincts), both Stalin and Brezhnev bequeathed to their successors an economy that was a shambles and a society ravaged by a host of ills. They also left it militarily strong and diplomatically on the offensive.

Both Khrushchev and Gorbachev immediately proposed to address a wide variety of domestic problems. Surely, the lessons of Khrushchev's experiments with a variety of economic stratagems and his lackadaisical attempts at greater permissiveness and tolerance after decades of Stalin's police and prisons have not been lost on Gorbachev. Khrushchev's successes and failures—to say nothing of his ultimate fate, his

Maurice Friedberg is head of the Department of Slavic Languages and Literatures at the University of Illinois.

ouster at the hand of his own associates—suggest a bewildering variety of practical constraints and tradeoffs, not to mention those imposed by the ideological parameters of a state dedicated to the communist idea. Understandably, any Soviet leader—and especially one whose background is primarily that of a Party functionary, as is Gorbachev's—would be loathe to resort to drastic changes of an indisputably systemic nature that would expose him to charges of doctrinal heresy and betrayal, and would prefer first to exhaust less drastic alternatives. Past experience, however, suggests that the latter are all too often inadequate to deal with the ingrained, deep-seated problems of a huge country made further immobile by an understandably passive citizenry and a mammoth state bureaucracy that overlaps with a Party apparatus of similar dimensions, to say nothing of special-interest groups that often conflict but must all somehow be appeased or at least neutralized.

In an attempt to assess the state of the Soviet Union at the end of the second year of the Gorbachev administration (and thus also to gauge the prospects of alternative future policies and developments), a conference on Soviet society was convened by the Department of State at Airlie House, Virginia, in the autumn of 1986. The gathering, which was co-chaired by the editors of this volume, was attended by government specialists on Soviet affairs as well as academics representing a wide range of disciplines. The latter included American scholars as well as several recent émigrés from the USSR. The papers selected for publication here are those that focused most directly on current trends, but they reflect also the presentations and comments of the other conference participants.

No attempt was made to evaluate the diplomatic dimensions of the present condition of the USSR. However, nearly every other aspect of Soviet domestic affairs was addressed directly or obliquely, thus providing a careful and detailed appraisal of the Soviet Union as of the end of 1986.

The state of the Soviet family seldom commands newspaper headlines in the West. In New York and Paris and London it is the news of Soviet dissidents, of literary sensations, and of restrictions on the sale of vodka that dominate dispatches from Moscow. Soviet media, for all their relative liveliness today, are also, understandably, preoccupied with personnel changes and official pronouncements by Gorbachev and his associates.

The family, however, is the molecule of a society. Even in Soviet conditions, it remains a "private" institution that may harbor, foster, and perpetuate values at variance with those of society at large. Hence, Soviet attitudes toward the family have been ambivalent over the years, at times hostile, at times friendly. The Soviet family today, while still to all appearances a solid enough institution (90 percent of the Soviet population, Mark Field indicates, lives in family units), is beset by grave tensions, not unlike those that American families face. Foremost among these is divorce. While still lower than the American, the Soviet divorce rate in 1984 was *thirteen times higher* than in 1950. Roughly half of Soviet marriages now end in divorce, about 800,000 annually, and fewer than half of the divorced women will remarry. Men blame the breakup of their marriages on incompatibility, while women cite alcoholism. Illegitimacy is rampant, with about a million children born annually out of wedlock. This, according to Field, may be a contributing factor to the very high infant mortality rate—about three times as high as in the United States. The high incidence of illegitimacy is also certainly a consequence of the primitive nature of Soviet contraceptive devices. The pill is still largely unavailable, and the crude and thick condoms are lovingly called "galoshes." As a result, abortions are often the birth-control method of *first* resort. About 80 percent of all pregnancies end in abortion—which was illegal as recently as 1955. In the past such evidence of social pathology was rarely if ever discussed in public or in the mass media. The subject is now in the open, one of the first beneficiaries of Gorbachev's *glasnost'*, or openness.

The single most critical issue that Gorbachev faces is the overall state of the Soviet national economy. Long stagnant, inefficient and technologically backward, that economy is now only beginning, so to speak, to be dragged, kicking and screaming, into the last quarter of the twentieth century. A measure of success is already being noted, and in any case, for all of its shortcomings, the USSR does not appear to face imminent economic collapse. As Vladimir Kontorovich notes, "Command economy is a viable system. While it cannot solve its immanent problems, it can prevent them from getting out of hand." In short, the Soviet economy can be fully expected to muddle through for many years to come. Still, the difficulties it faces are formidable. Take, for instance, the unequal distribution of labor. There is overpopulation in the Central Asian republics, where relatively few major industrial enterprises are located, but the Muslim population there appears quite unwilling to move to areas with serious labor shortage. Whether attractive inducements would bring about a change in these attitudes cannot be predicted.

The Soviet labor force includes an inordinate number of "poorly trained and poorly paid" specialists. Kontorovich believes that "there is often not enough work" to keep these specialists busy, which in turn means "that money spent on their education and wages is wasted." The waste is compounded by the fact that many of these mediocre specialists, disheartened by prospects for the future, become blue-collar workers. Blair Ruble informed the conference that Soviet legislation of the late 1970s and early '80s "imposed tougher sanctions against labor discipline violations, rolled back job protection rights, strengthened job placement mechanisms and reoriented incentive structures around a perceived need to increase labor productivity." As Kontorovich reminds us, however, such measures cannot be carried too far: "Labor shortages make it impossible to institute a discipline campaign for workers as effective as that for managers. Excess demand for labor is one of the main causes of deterioration of labor discipline, increasing incidence of absenteeism, and general decline in effort exerted at the workplace."

Any reform exacts a price, and would-be labor reformers must be mindful of the tradeoffs and constraints involved. More independence for managers invites worker apathy. Greater financial incentives risk inflating wage differentials, and, conversely, egalitarian wage policies reward low productivity. The outlook, therefore, while not alarming, is decidedly bleak. In Kontorovich's view, "Success of Gorbachev's labor policies will not mean balancing demand and supply for labor, or providing workers with strong incentives. The very nature of command economy breeds shortages. The Soviet economy (like any large hierarchical organization) has trouble providing high-powered incentives. These problems cannot be resolved within the confines of the current system."

No initiative of Gorbachev has attracted as much attention both at home and abroad as his resolute drive to stamp out alcoholism. But then, it may be argued, no other government drive in recent memory has so directly affected nearly every Soviet family. The highlights of that campaign (long overdue, in the opinion of most observers) are presented in Vladimir Treml's paper. By the autumn of 1986 vodka had been made prohibitively expensive—18.5 rubles, or roughly two days' wages, per liter (at the same time imbibers were tempted by cheap soft drinks). Fines for alcohol-related offenses became downright draconian, and stringent limits were imposed on amounts of liquor sold to customers and on times when the sale of alcohol is permitted. Yet, as

Treml emphasizes, there was "relatively little in the way of positive steps" that would make cutting down alcohol consumption (much less total abstinence) easier, in spite of tacit recognition that a lack of entertainment and recreation facilities contributes to the allure of alcohol. So far, there are only *promises* of more athletic equipment, gardening tools, and necessities for other hobbies. But the simple fact is that the alcohol crisis in the Soviet Union had reached catastrophic dimensions. Horrendous alcohol consumption (15 liters annually per person over fifteen years of age, of which two-thirds was *vodka*—unlike elsewhere in the world, where alcohol is primarily wine or beer, with lower alcoholic content) had contributed, between the 1960s and early 1980s, to a *decline* of life expectancy among males by four years. Fully one-fifth of all deaths in the country were alcohol-related. No wonder, Treml believes, that the alcoholic calamity has encouraged even such entirely unrealistic goals as total abstinence.

In his conversations with writers in the summer of 1986, Gorbachev pointed out that alcoholism, the scourge of the Slavs, has begun to make inroads even among the Central Asians—an oblique way of recognizing the price of religious assimilation: in the past, abstemious Islamic codes of behavior had protected Muslims from this particular pestilence. But, as Paul Goble points out in his paper on Soviet nationalities, acculturation does not affect ethnic identity. Indeed, "leaders of successful ethnic political challenges and anticolonial movements have almost always come not from the most backward, but from the most assimilated groups." Moreover, Goble explains, in the USSR nowadays minority nationalism is not primarily attachment to traditions, but rather competition with Russians (or other Soviet ethnic groups) for good jobs and scarce resources. In all likelihood, then, nationalist tensions will become exacerbated, as the non-Slavs, who in 1959 were a *tenth* of the country's population, become a *fifth* in 1989. Of the non-Slavs, it is the Muslim populations that are the fastest growing. Yet, as already mentioned, they cannot be induced to move to areas where serious labor shortages exist, and achievement of a certain level of facility with the Russian language appears to have made no dent in the Muslims' sense of ethnic identity. In fact, Goble believes, "the rise in Russian language knowledge has made it more likely that non-Russians can and will compete with Russians for jobs and resources and that their national identities will be intensified, and national sensitivities exacerbated in the process." The more so, since Gorbachev is perceived as favoring the Russians. That this ostensible favoritism is

xii   MAURICE FRIEDBERG

rooted in objective economic reasons does not change the perception.

One is intrigued by the fact that Goble's argument finds support in Anthony Olcott's paper, which deals with cultural developments. In Olcott's view, Russified non-Russians will inevitably become more prominent in Russian culture. One example is the writer Chinghiz Aitmatov, a Kirghiz, who is now, arguably, the most prominent *Russian* novelist. There was some grumbling about the propriety of this "Muslim" author's portrayal of Christ-like personages and Christian seminarians in his recent novel *The Execution Block*. That neither the author, nor most of his critics, were religious believers, compounds the paradox of the situation.

The Gorbachev era has seen the publication of many authors and titles long suppressed—although, one may add, nearly always on condition that the authors be safely dead. As for literary sensations, these have been mostly exposés of Stalinist crimes, as in Anatolii Rybakov's forthcoming *Children of the Arbat*, or of abuses in the present. Two examples of the latter are Valentin Rasputin's *The Fire* and Victor Astaf'ev's *The Sad Detective*, which portray the squalor of the Soviet provinces, greed, corruption, and crime. Because both categories of writing are so much more truthful and frank in their treatment of social reality, Olcott observes, it is "tempting to conclude . . . that the Gorbachev era will be one of cultural achievement and latitude." That may well be so, Olcott argues, but literature's *influence* will decline. Already now, people in the Soviet Union are reading less than in the past, and then primarily for entertainment. The lessons of "truthful" descriptions of social pathology are likely to be lost on people intent on finding diversion and not instruction. At present, according to Olcott, "the most popular books [in the USSR] are detective novels, science fiction, and thrillers, while horror and sex have begun to emerge as genres." Western perceptions of Soviet culture are based almost exclusively on contacts with elite culture, which may be appealing to the intelligentsia but is not socially influential. On the other hand, popular Soviet culture—the artistic sustenance, such as it is, of the Soviet masses—is hardly known abroad. Foreigners, for instance, know Soviet classical music, but not Soviet rock-and-roll. They know the *avant garde* Taganka theater, but hardly anyone abroad is interested in the average Soviet theater, which "is required to put on four plays a year, one industrial, one international, one about Lenin, and one 'highly desirable,' a classic."

Soviet citizens may be reading less, but they are watching more television. By 1986, 93 percent of the country's population had access to television, Ellen Mickiewicz informs us in her essay; in 1960 only five percent had TV. Television appears to be the most important source of not only information but also, and increasingly, entertainment. Curiously, the radio is staging a comeback of sorts, and radio listeners are likely to be young and better educated: "It is the transmitting of relatively fast-breaking news, both foreign and domestic, and heavy programming of more up-to-date pop music that has attracted a growing audience."

The USSR has also at its disposal one mass medium peculiar to it alone, namely the tens of thousands of "Znanie" (Knowledge) Society lecturers whose semicaptive audiences receive information and editorial comment on subjects ranging from Communist Party doctrine and international affairs to art history and medical advice.

One area of communications technology that is still in its infancy in the USSR is the video cassette recorder. Mickiewicz suggests that this may be in part a reflection of the authorities' ambivalence about their desirability: video cassettes, it is feared, may be used to smuggle into the USSR recorded pornography or politically subversive material. At present, only 4,000 VCRs are produced annually, but very rapid expansion is planned: 60,000 are to be manufactured in 1990.

This, then, was roughly the condition of Soviet society as it entered the third year of the Gorbachev administration. It is, obviously, a society in flux. Gorbachev's spectacular activism affects, in one way or another, every Soviet citizen's working conditions, leisure time, shelter, and food (especially drink). We must not, however, be deceived by the glitter of changes, for in the long run most of Gorbachev's reforms—like scores of reforms before them—are likely to be vitiated by many factors. They may be brought to nought, whether by the inertia or resistance of special-interest groups, or because they are contraindicated by other, equally valid considerations; by economic, military, and social constraints; by the limitations of communist dogma (which may be stretched but not broken); or, finally, by the sheer immobilism of a colossal country that, for all the decades of revolutionary rhetoric, distrusts innovation. The bewildering heterogeneity of a country that has over a quarter of a billion population living in eleven time zones, with often clashing economic needs, real and perceived, argues for the least controversial and painful of compromises, that of continued immobilism and stagnation. These have some impressive virtues. They are accepted, if only tacitly, by most, and they are reassuring, if only

through their familiarity. It may not be entirely accidental that one of
the most idiosyncratic great novels in world literature, a stunning study
of passivity and sloth as a philosophy of life, Ivan Goncharov's *Oblomov*, was written by a Russian.

Nor must we lose sight of what is self-evident. There are no reasons
to doubt Mikhail Gorbachev's devotion to the communist cause. However sincere his desire for change, his concern for the welfare of his
people and for the strength of his nation, he is not likely to promulgate
changes that would in any way alter the essence of the Soviet character
of the country he rules.

Soviet Society Under Gorbachev

THE CONTEMPORARY SOVIET FAMILY: PROBLEMS, ISSUES, PERSPECTIVES

Mark G. Field

Dynasties, societies, and empires have turned to dust when the family within them began to disintegrate. . . . Dynasties, societies, and empires that do not create families or that destroy family stability begin to boast of their progress and rattle their weapons; in dynasties, empires, and societies where the family fell to pieces, so too did commonality; evil began to overwhelm good. . . .

Viktor Astaf'ev, *The Sad Detective*[1]

Introduction

In the complex equation that sums up, however imperfectly, the strengths, weaknesses, resilience, and prospects of Soviet society, no variable is more important or decisive than its human resources. Alongside natural and economic wealth and the general state of knowledge and technology, human beings in the final analysis constitute the decisive factor. Any assessment of the Soviet Union must therefore encompass both the quantitative aspects of that resource (the size of the population, its age and sex composition, its natural increase, its urban/rural distribution, the number of people in the work force, and so on) and its qualitative characteristics (its education, attitudes, morale, general views of the regime, manner of raising children, and so on). A critical initial role, both in the reproduction of the population and in its quality, is played by the family, a basic unit of social structure that is entrusted with several critical functions. As we shall see, the overwhelming majority of the Soviet people live within family units. The

Mark G. Field is professor of sociology at Boston University.

family therefore deserves our close attention, particularly at a time of rapid and often traumatizing social change such as we are witnessing today in Gorbachev's Soviet Union.

In this kind of examination, we must note that the family has been changing and has been affected by modernization and development all around the world. In this respect, the Soviet Union is no exception, and by looking at other societies we can learn and understand a great deal of what has happened there and is happening today as a result of the shifting of economic activities from the land to industry, from the village to the city. (According to some sociologists, the rapidity of rural-urban population shifts in the Soviet Union in the last few years is "transforming the country's social structure as none of the wars or internal conflicts of this century have changed it."[2]) At the same time, there are some aspects of the family situation that are rather peculiar to the Soviet Union (and Soviet-type societies), and these aspects deserve close attention. In the USSR the family has been the object of close ideological definition and scrutiny as well as the target of official public policy and social concern to a degree that would not be conceivable in pluralistic systems in the West. In the latter societies it is generally held that interference of the state in family affairs is usually not warranted; that the family is an area of intense personal and private concern (epitomized by the English saying that one's home is a castle that even the king dare not enter without permission); and that the role of the polity in this context should be marginal or residual, not central. It is true, of course, that in such societies increasingly the state does affect the family, although usually indirectly, through specific measures such as taxation, income support, food stamps, and so on. In the Soviet Union, on the other hand, the family has been "an object of public policy from the start, and its transformation was viewed as a necessary condition of altering patterns of participation and authority in the wider society."[3]

This is a propitious moment to cast a retrospective look at the family in the Soviet Union, to examine some of the major problems and issues that have emerged, to follow the debates in official circles and in the media, and to hazard some tentative guesses as to the prospects for the Soviet family.

In addition to demographic background data indicating significant trends, we will examine some aspects of the Soviet family's performance of its roles in society. The first of these is *socialization*, i.e., the initial care and upbringing of the child from the moment of birth on—a function traditionally assigned to the family. Socialization entails the critical task of transmitting to the future generation the nongenetic inheritance of society—its language, culture, values, norms, collective memory, and so on. The physical reproduction of the population is never sufficient to ensure the continuity of social structures. There are, of course, many other agencies of socialization in Soviet society (for example, nurseries, daycare centers, schools, Party youth organizations, peer and work groups), but the family is important because the *initial* process of socialization usually takes place within it. What happens when the infant is helpless and very impressionable tends to leave its stamp for the balance of the individual's life.

In the process of socialization, we may distinguish upbringing from education. Upbringing, the major task of the family, is the conveying to the infant, child, and adolescent of the basic and general aspects of culture just mentioned, while education is more concerned with specific knowledge and skills of the type that are necessary for adult functioning and work. As time goes by, education becomes an increasingly important component of socialization.

A second issue is the role that the family plays in society *for its adult members*. Generally speaking, the family is the basic social unit of society (the germ cell, as Soviet contemporary ideologues like to call it); it is the setting in which most people live, rest, and procreate. As such, the family provides a basic psychological, emotional, and social anchorage point. It is the place to which one goes when there is nowhere else to go, it is the locus of nonoccupational activities, of affective and sexual life, it is where one's emotional batteries are recharged (or, in a troubled family, depleted). It is a place away from public life and the demands of the workplace, where the "mask" that people feel they must wear in public encounters can be safely dropped. It is, in other words, a private place for its adult members just as it is a "nest" for its dependent children.

Because of the close integration between the family and other social units, as people daily shuttle between the family and other settings (the job or the school) it is reasonable to assume that what transpires in one setting is never completely irrelevant to the others. Thus, worries about the situation at work may have their repercussions at home, just as the concerns of a mother about her child's health may well leave her distracted and inattentive at work. The moods, dispositions, and attitudes of adult family members affect the way they relate to their children and each other, and thus inevitably influence the home atmosphere, including the socialization process. When we deal with the family, in its multiple facets and functions, we are dealing with a critical subsystem of social structure. There is constant interrelation between the social system as a whole and its subsystems, such that they are "organically" related to each other and not encapsulated from each other: what happens in one is bound to affect the other, and *vice versa*. Thus, the family both reflects social change and is a cause of social change, in an endless chain of causality.

A sociological conceptualization of the family

The family, as a special type of human grouping, stands at the intersection of the biological and the social. In the most general terms, a family is made up of individuals who are held together by bonds of solidarity based on sexual access or biological descent or relatedness. The typical urban family of today (sometimes called the nuclear or conjugal family) usually consists of two adult members (the married couple) and their dependent children. There is a network of mutual obligations, reflecting that solidarity mentioned earlier, which mandates a special concern for each other on the part of the married partners, as well as obligations toward their dependents (or nonadult children) and their own parents. That sense of obligation is held to be stronger and more valid than for other individuals outside the family. Family institutions also regulate sexual access by specifying who may and who may not be considered an acceptable marriage partner.

The bonds of solidarity and mutual obligation established between parents and their children certainly are based initially on the biological relationship, but that relationship is only a structural point of departure. The nature of the relationship between a parent and a child, like that between the spouses, is *sociological*. Society and culture define the obligations that family members have toward each other, and this relationship may exist in the absence of any biological relatedness, as in the case of adoptive or foster parents. The family is responsible not only for reproduction, but also for the protection of the helpless child and for the early socialization of that child. The early "launching" of the individual into his life orbit is the major task of the family.

It is the prospect that a couple will have children that makes marriage such an important societal institution. It accounts for its legal nature and the obligations it entails, and the fact that in most past societies and in some today it is also sanctioned by a religious (not only civil) consecration. The Soviet Union has recognized the importance of marriage, and has made the wedding ceremony a symbolic occasion that to some extent is endowed with the same emotional content as a religious service. In a sociological sense, a married couple without children is not a family. This has also been recognized by the Soviets in that divorce between consenting spouses without children is an almost automatic process.

In the preindustrial age the family was a much larger group than what is typical today in industrial societies. The extended family, most common in agricultural societies, usually consisted of three generations and collateral relatives. In fact, in the past, the extended family was often *the* society for the individual. It had many functions that today have been spun off; it was, first, an economic unit that extracted from the soil the necessary sustenance for survival. Family members (even children) were seen as important sources of labor in the struggle for survival. The family might also be a religious unit. A distinctive style of life and patterns of authority are associated with this kind of family— sometime called the "patriarchal" or "traditional" family in the Soviet and Russian contexts.

Today the Soviet family, small in size and usually two-generational, tends to be primarily a consumption unit, and the economic activities of its members tend to be played *outside* the family. Fundamental in an understanding of family problems in the Soviet Union today (as elsewhere in the industrial world) is the split between the home and the job, between the household and the occupational sphere. This did not exist in the past when the members of the family, in fact, lived and worked *on* the "means of production"—the land. This split led to a differentiation of sex roles, with the male typically leaving the household to work while the woman stayed home to take care of the household and the children. But this neat division of labor is, in many instances, and in the Soviet Union in particular, now more the exception than the rule. For economic, as well as for ideological and political reasons, the Soviet regime has encouraged women to also hold jobs outside the home. Originally, this was meant as a policy to liberate women from domesticity and subjugation to the male. The Soviet regime tried to make political hay from the fact that it was enfranchising members of the population who, under the previous regime, lacked freedom and economic independence. But this ideologically and politically motivated move coincided with a voracity on the part of the Soviet regime for manpower (or should we say womanpower) to work in its expanding economy. In the Soviet Union, women do not constitute a labor reserve, to be drawn upon in special cases: women are a critical and indispensable component of the labor force. The large-scale employment of women as a major labor resource has led to acute problems and stresses, as women attempt to combine (or juggle) domestic and occupational roles. The situation has no exact parallel in the case of men who, in the majority of cases, feel that their occupational role is most important and that household functions should be performed by the woman as a "natural" extension of her child-bearing functions as in the traditional and extended family, and this in spite of the fact that she usually has a full-time job as demanding as her husband's.

Today's Soviet husband is no more a patriarchal dictator. His authority has been eroded in the face of the far greater economic independence gained by women through employment. The role of women is extremely difficult, given the often conflicting obligations of home, child care, and the job; indeed, this is one of the major stress points in Soviet society today. On the other hand, women have gained freedom to marry whom they please (or not to marry), to have or not to have children, and to opt out of marriage through divorce or separation. The regime has sought, at times, to limit these freedoms, for example by prohibiting abortions or making divorces difficult and expensive to obtain. At the present time, these limitations are minimal (too minimal in the eyes of some). The situation is one of potential, if not actual, conflict, a kind of guerrilla war of the sexes that contributes to the instability of the small, structurally unsupported Soviet urban family. The impact of such a situation, both on the socializing and protection functions of the family for their young and on the personal adjustment of the adult population, is far from trivial. It affects, for instance, the reproductive functions of the family. In many areas, the birthrate is practically equal, if not inferior, to the mortality rate, leading to concerns about the replacement of the population, never mind its growth. Given the need for the employment of women, the many problems associated with the chronic housing shortage and consequent lack of privacy, the shortage of labor-saving appliances, the difficulties associated with shopping, the unwillingness of husbands to pitch in with household chores, it is hardly surprising that one witnesses not only a rising divorce rate but also an unwillingness on the part of Soviet women (particularly in the European part of the country) to bear more than one child (if any).

It should be noted that these characterizations do not seem to apply to the populations of the Central Asian and the Transcaucasian republics, to which we will refer henceforth as the "Southern Tier." These are areas where the traditional cultures, and the lower levels of industrialization and urbanization, have contributed to keeping the family fairly strong and productive of children. It may be expected that gradually, as these areas become subject to the same structural changes brought about by industrialization and urban living, families will become smaller and less fertile. But for the time being, the difference in the reproduction rates of the Southern Tier areas and the rest of the Soviet Union suggests an alteration in the Soviet ethnic balance in favor of the population from that tier. This trend has significant implications for the future social and ethnic makeup of the Soviet Union—the composition of the labor force, the military, and the party—and eventually for the political authority of Moscow. The nationality problem is not the central issue of this paper, but, to the degree that differential fertility rates between the Slavic and Baltic areas and the Southern Tier are a reflection of family patterns, they should be kept in mind as background when interpreting official policy and pronouncements on the family. A delicate question, for instance, is whether the Soviet Union will modulate its family policy to encourage an increase in the birthrate in the Slavic and Baltic areas and a decrease in the Southern Tier without violating the officially mandated prescription of the equality of nationalities. Some proposals to that effect have, indeed, been floated, although of course they do not specifically mention a concern about ethnic balance.

These then are, in broad strokes, some of the major issues that we will examine in some detail below. Of course, the regime has a host of other concerns on its agenda, from the faltering economy to the international situation and the arms race. But judging from the amount of attention paid in the media to the family, the increasing divorce rate, young people and their interests and motivations, the complaints of women, the disappearance of the traditional baby sitter in the person of the grandmother or *babushka*, and many other related issues, there is little doubt that an inquiry into the Soviet family will yield important insights into the nature of the Soviet social order and possible directions for the future.

Family policy in the Soviet Union

The Marxist (and Engelsian) interpretation of the family provided the departure point for early Soviet family legislation and policies. The official view was that the institution of the family under capitalism was based primarily on private property, and produced, among other things, an unjust inequality among the sexes. At one point, Engels stated that this inequality between the sexes was the prototype of the class struggle between two unequals. This inequality derived from the fact that men "owned" women as their private means for the production of legitimate (male) offspring to whom their property could be passed. Marriage, that most intimate of all human relationships, was determined by the parents of the marriage pair (on the basis again of property considerations) and love or mutual attraction played no role in marriage formation. Obsessed by the fear that their property might go on to "illegitimate" heirs, men established the bondage of women to ensure that any offspring would be their own. This led then to a double standard: enforced monogamy for women and philandering for men (thereby encouraging prostitution) and a stigmatization of women who bore children out of wedlock (adulteresses) and of such children themselves (bastards).

Whatever the validity of Engels's views, early Soviet policies were aimed at righting these wrongs and at facilitating the transfer of the care, education, and maintenance of children from the home to the society. An important reason for that policy, in addition to its ideological origins, was the attempt on the part of the regime to appeal to those individuals who, under the previous order, were seen as having been victims of discrimination: women, children born out of wedlock, minorities, the young, and the poor. It was an attempt to subvert traditional patterns of authority, and to gather the loyalty and support of those who had been downtrodden in the past. This meant, in effect, transferring most socialization functions away from the family, and removing the child from the presumably conservative, if not reactionary and counterrevolutionary, influence of the traditional patriarchal family to a setting in which he could be socialized according to the needs of the new regime.

This policy was also said to liberate woman from the yoke of her husband (or her father) by enabling her (by freeing her of domestic and childrearing tasks) to support herself through her own work, securing her economic independence and thus true equality. This also meant the end of the difference between a registered (legal) marriage and an unregistered one (common-law marriage). It also was meant to erase the stigmatizing differentiation between legitimate and illegitimate children. But this did not necessarily mean the end of the "family''in every sense of the word: it meant the end of the traditional and "reactionary'' family tied to private property. From now on, men and women could live together. The couple would be the new family, linked by bonds of love, mutual attraction, and compatibility. A "marriage'' would be the result of mutual selection, and not of parental arrangements based on cold economic calculations. The "family'' would survive as long as "love'' lasted. When and if that state of bliss came to an end, unilaterally or bilaterally, the marriage would be dissolved automatically, and there would not be complications brought about by questions of child guardianship, alimony, and allocation of property, since children would be taken care by the society through state-provided institutions.

This early Soviet legislation was easily the most radical of its kind. Marriage consisted of a simple registration at the civil registry, divorce was the result of a declaration by one of the spouses, the distinction between "natural'' and legitimate children disappeared as a legal category, and abortions on nonmedical or social grounds were legalized.

The results of these steps were less than promising. For one, the young Soviet state, beset by a multiplicity of problems, was in no position to fulfill the conditions that Engels had specified for extra-familial socialization: it lacked the funds, the will, and the personnel to take on this responsibility. In addition, the regime's family policies had their impact primarily on the urban areas, where only about one-fifth of the population resided, leaving the countryside practically unaffected. Yet, even the limited results of the new family policies were sufficient to show that their continuation and extension would directly conflict with, and cripple, the ambitious programs of forced draft industrialization launched by Stalin at the end of the 1920s. In particular, the encouragement of the dissolution of the traditional family, and the absence of reasonably effective alternate sources of socialization, meant the growth of a new generation, unguided, undisciplined, and unfit intellectually and emotionally to help in building a new society based on personal sacrifice and discipline, punctuality and accuracy, steadiness and perseverance. As the family became unglued or weakened, many children were left to the noxious influences of the street and juvenile gangs that encouraged hooliganism and undermined whatever influence the school system had upon these children and future "builders of communism.''

The thirties saw an 180-degree turn in the regime's attitude and policies toward the family and children. Parallel measures were also to strengthen the family and to make divorces more and more difficult. Later there were measures to encourage (or at least support) mothers of children born out of wedlock, a step taken toward the end of World War II due to the concern raised by the enormous male losses in the war, the resulting unhinging of the sex ratio in favor of men, and the implications of these events for the national birthrate. The policy of unrestricted abortion was eliminated in 1936 despite widespread public discussion indicating that the public wanted to retain abortion.

There was, to be sure, some liberalization of family policies after Stalin's death in 1953. It became easier to obtain divorces, abortions were again permitted on nontherapeutic grounds (1955), and certain kinds of paternity suits were reinstated (1965 and 1968). But the family, as now constituted in the Soviet Union, seems to present profound dilemmas for the regime, and the regime does not quite know what to do about it, particularly in view of the often contradictory demands it continues to make on the family. It wants (and needs) women to continue working outside the home, to keep the household as a social unit to socialize the young, and to bear more than a single child, and it wants men to assume at least some childrearing responsibilities and household functions despite their legendary reluctance to do so. Yet it fails to provide convenient and efficient services or to build enough housing to permit "normal" family life and some modicum of privacy. This then is the background of the situation today, which some Soviet authors themselves describe in terms of crisis. As one of the Soviet Union's leading demographers sums it up, "Today's young family is full of conflict, unstable and with few children."[4]

The demographic situation in the 1980s

Whatever can be said about the imperiled nature of the Soviet family, the fact remains that the overwhelming majority of the Soviet population lives in family units. In 1970 there were 58.7 million families, embracing over nine-tenths of the population. The 1979 census figures indicated there were over 66 million families early in 1979, over 42 million of which lived in the cities, and close to 24 million in the rural areas. Close to 90 percent of the urban population and slightly over 90 percent of the rural population were members of families.

The Soviet Union has become, in the last few years, an essentially *urban* society since almost twice as many live in such surroundings as live in the villages. The rapidity of the urbanization of the Soviet Union after World War II, and particularly since the death of Stalin, is one important factor that has changed the nature of the Soviet family and contributed to the multiplicity of issues and problems that affect it today. In the twenty-five years between 1961 and 1986, the urban population grew from 50 to 65.6 percent of the total. This meant an absolute increase of *about 75 million* people living in urban surround-ings, or an average annual increase in the urban population of about three million.[5] According to an interview with demographer Viktor Perevedentsev in 1985, the overall number of people migrating to the cities annually is between 3 and 4 million, with 1.5 to 2 million moving in the other direction, for a net annual shift of 1.5 to 2 million people to the cities each year at the present time.

This migration has two distinct components: in the Slavic and Baltic areas of the Soviet Union, where a stable rural workforce is needed and where the cities are filling their manpower needs primarily through normal growth, some 25 people per 1,000 leave the countryside for the cities annually. In Central Asia, on the other hand, only 4 per 1,000 leave their rural homes each year. Perevedentsev adds that while the rural population in northern Russia has been cut in half in the last 25 years, it has more than doubled in Central Asia.

According to the 1979 census two-thirds of all Soviet families con-sisted of a married couple with or without children (Table 1). Eight percent of the families consisted of a married couple (with or without children) with the parent of one of the spouses living with them, and another 5 percent were the same type of family but with other relatives living with them (as close to an extended family as is likely to be found in the Soviet Union). Twelve percent of all families (12.5 percent in the cities, 10.6 percent in the countryside) were single-parent families consisting of a mother (or in very rare cases a father) and children.

As might be expected, the Soviet family is small. For the whole of the Soviet Union, the average family size in 1979 was 3.5 (down from 3.7 in 1970), with a range from 2.3 for single-parent families in the cities to a high of 6.9 for extended families in the countryside. These extended families are found primarily in the Southern Tier, where the family size may be considerably greater than the average indicated here. But the percentage that these families represent in the total is, as we have seen, very small.

The average family size of 3.5 conceals important internal differ-ences. For the nation as a whole, four-fifths of urban families and two-

Table 1

Distribution of Soviet Families by Type, 1979, Urban and Rural

	Number of families	Percentage of each type	Average family size
USSR			
All families[1]	66,307,213	100	3.5
consisting of:			
a married couple with or without children	43,827,022	66	3.3
a married couple with or without children, with a parent of a spouse	5,405,664	8	4.6
a married couple with or without children, with (or without) a parent of a spouse, with other relatives	3,385,192	5	4.8
two or more married couples with or without children, with (or without) a parent of a spouse, with (or without) other relatives	2,826,997	3.5	6.3
a mother (or father) with children	7,857,003	12	2.4
unaccounted[2]	3,006,335	4.5	—
Urban population			
All families[1]	42,440,151	100	3.3
consisting of:			
a married couple with or without children	28,058,835	67	3.2
a married couple with or without children, with a parent of a spouse	3,203,864	7.5	4.3
a married couple with or without children, with (or without) a parent of a spouse, with other relatives	2,130,568	5.0	4.6
two or more married couples with or without children, with (or without) a parent of a spouse, with (or without) other relatives	1,753,035	4.0	5.9
a mother (or father) with children	5,316,738	12.5	2.3
unaccounted[2]	1,977,111	4.6	—
Rural population			
All families[1]	23,867,062	100	3.8
consisting of:			
a married couple with or without children	15,767,187	66	3.6
a married couple with or without children, with a parent of a spouse	2,201,800	9	5.0
a married couple with or without children, with (or without) a parent of a spouse, with other relatives	1,254,624	5	5.2
two or more married couples with or without children, with (or without) a parent of a spouse, with (or without) other relatives	1,073,962	4.5	6.9
a mother (or father) with children	2,540,265	10.6	2.6
unaccounted[2]	1,029,224	4.3	—

1. Included in the families are children of all ages living with their parents.
2. Residuals.

Source: Tsentral'noe Statisticheskoe Upravlenie SSSR, *Chislennost' i sostav naseleniia SSSR: Po dannym Vsesoiuznoi perepisi naseleniia 1979 goda* (Moscow: Finansy i statistika, 1984), Table 51, p. 253.

thirds of rural families had two to four members, but in the Southern Tier at least 70 percent of the families had four or more members. Regional differences *increased* between the 1959, 1970, and 1979 censuses. Although the overall family size in the Soviet Union remains fairly constant from year to year (with a slight decrease), this constancy is the product of two widely differing phenomena—a decrease in the size of the family in the western part of the Soviet Union, areas that are increasingly urban, and an increase in the Southern Tier where the population is still heavily engaged in agricultural pursuits, and where the traditional family is still very much the cultural norm and shows relatively great stability over time.

There is of course no telling what will happen to that Southern Tier when the process of urbanization and modernization takes a firm hold, as it is bound to. There is little reason to expect that the traditional family, even in the face of a culture that upholds strong family ties and stability, will be able to withstand intact the process of moving to the cramped quarters of Soviet cities. But for the time being, and probably for the duration of Gorbachev's rule, the striking difference between these two types of family is likely to remain visible. It will, as pointed out earlier, lead to an increase in the proportion the Southern Tier population represents in the total Soviet population. It is thus plausible that in the distant future the differences that now exist between the families in the Southern Tier and the other areas of the Soviet Union (differences that to some degree also reflect the rural vs. urban way of life) will gradually disappear as the Soviet Union becomes more and more urbanized and industrialized. Such a situation, as far as we can make any judgment, will only contribute to perpetuating the problems of the family in terms of both its decreased fertility and increased instability, with all the consequences that these have for its functions of providing a comfortable and stable home for its members, and particularly its children.

It should also be noted that of those who live outside of a family (about 11 percent of the population in 1979), about half were over the age of 60, and of these about three-fourths were women. Thus for the majority of those who live outside of a family, the reason may be not deliberate choice but circumstances such as the death of a spouse or the lack of available marriage partners.

The data in Table 1 give some indication of the distribution of the types of Soviet families, as well as an average number of family members for each type. More precise information on the distribution of

Table 2

Distribution of Families in the USSR by the Number of People Living Together, 1970 and 1979, per 1000 Families

USSR	2 persons	3 persons	4 persons	5 persons	6 persons	7 persons	8 persons	9 persons	10 or more persons	average no. of persons per family
Urban and rural population										
1970	254	262	241	126	59	28	15	8	7	3.7
1979	297	289	230	95	41	20	12	7	9	3.5
Urban population										
1970	252	303	266	111	40	14	7	4	3	3.5
1979	291	322	249	85	29	11	6	3	4	3.3
Rural population										
1970	257	205	206	146	86	46	27	15	12	4.0
1979	306	230	196	113	62	36	23	15	19	3.8

Source: Tsentral'noe Statisticheskoe Upravlenie SSSR, *Chislennost' i sostav naseleniia SSSR: Po dannym Vsesoiuznoi perepisi naseleniia 1979 goda*, p. 222.

all families, regardless of type, by the number of people living in each household may be gathered from Table 2. This table shows, in general, that the proportion of small families (3 members or less) increased during the 1970s, while the proportion of large families (with the exception of those with 10 or more members) decreased. By the way, the proportion of very large families (10 and more) was less than one percent in 1979. The large, extended family is certainly not the Soviet modal type.

We have mentioned the fact that in the Soviet Union marriage is the preferred way of life. And indeed, the data suggest that in the course of time, the marriage rate (as expressed, for example, in the number of marriages per 1,000 of the population per year) has remained fairly steady since the early '70s at around 10. In fact, the latest piece of data we have shows a rate of 10.8. And yet, a glance at the rate of registered divorce shows not steadiness but a steady increase, and this trend has

Soviet commentators considerably concerned. In 1950, the first postwar year for which such data are available, the divorce rate was 0.4/1,000 as against a marriage rate of 11.6/1,000. There were 32 divorces per 1,000 marriages. In 1984, the last year for which we have data, the divorce rate was 5.2/1,000 of the population as against a marriage rate of 10.8/1,000, showing that about half the marriages broke up. In total numbers, there were 2,634,000 registered marriages in 1984 and 932,000 registered divorces. In 1984 the divorce rate in terms of divorces per constant units of the population was 13 times greater than it had been in 1950. To some degree, however, the divorce explosion after 1965 may reflect the considerable easing of the procedure in that year. Under the legislation in force since 1944, divorce was difficult and expensive, which meant that many people who may have wanted to divorce were unable to do so. Since 1965 it has been simplified. For example, as was mentioned earlier, if both parties want a divorce and there are no children, it is granted almost automatically. A court procedure is mandated if the divorce is contested and if there are minor children.[6] The divorce figures for 1950 and 1960 probably underreported the degree of family instability and break-ups in those years, and the divorce explosion after 1965 may to some degree have been an artifact rather than a true measure of the increase in family instability. But what is no artifact is the contemporary divorce situation in which practically one marriage in two ends in divorce (see Table 3).

These are, of course, aggregate statistics that do not reflect geographical and cultural variations. Thus, in 1984 in Moscow there were 86,536 registered marriages and 44,554 divorces, giving a divorce/marriage ratio of 51 percent. In Erevan, the capital of Soviet Armenia, on the other hand, there were 10,840 marriages and 2,041 divorces. That ratio was only 20 percent, two and a half times smaller than in the Slavic and Baltic areas of the Soviet Union. An idea of regional variations can be obtained from Table 4, which provides marriage and divorce figures for 29 republican capitals and cities with over one million inhabitants.

Of the over 932,000 registered marriages that were dissolved in 1984, about 29 thousand (about 3 percent) foundered after less than one year. Most divorces took place after more than one year of marriage; the greatest number, 276,000 or about 3 percent, came after 5 to 9 years of married life. The largest number of divorces (250,000 for males, 242,000 for women) involved couples between the ages of 25 and 29. Greater detail on the fate of Soviet marriages (for 1984) can be found in

Table 3

Registered Marriages and Divorces, USSR, 1940–1984

Year	Registered marriages[a]		Registered divorces			U.S. Divorces per 1,000 population
	Number	Per 1,000 population	Number	Per 1,000 population	Per 1,000 marriages	
1940	1,228,793	6.3	205,605	1.1	167	2.0
1950	2,080,817	11.6	67,353	0.4	32	2.6
1960	2,591,509	12.1	270,227	1.3	104	2.2
1965	2,008,673	8.7	360,424	1.6	179	2.5
1966	2,087,599	8.9	646,095	2.8	309	—
1967	2,131,888	9.0	646,295	2.7	303	2.7
1970	2,365,259	9.7	636,232	2.6	269	2.9
1971	2,460,000	10.0	644,800	2.6	262	3.7[b]
1973	2,516,267	10.1	678,883	2.7	270	4.4
1974	2,606,700	10.3	743,400	2.9	285	4.5
1975	2,722,800	10.7	783,400	3.1	287	4.8
1976		10.1		3.4		
1980	2,724,600					
1984	2,634,100	10.8	932,800	5.2	354	5.0

a. Since these statistics do not distinguish first from subsequent marriages, the figures for marriage and divorce are not totally independent of each other. In 1973, 14.6 percent of males and 13 percent of females marrying had been married before; *Naselenie SSSR 1973*, p. 172.

b. 1972.

Sources: For 1940–1975, Gail Warshofsky Lapidus, *Women in Soviet Society: Equality, Development, and Social Change* (Berkeley: University of California Press, 1978), Table 30; Tsentral'noe Statisticheskoe Upravlenie, *Narodnoe khoziaistvo SSSR za 60 let* (Moscow, 1977), p. 74; Tsentral'noe Statisticheskoe Upravlenie, *Naselenie SSSR 1973. Statisticheskii sbornik* (Moscow, 1975), p. 150. For 1980, *Sbornik stat. materialov, 1981* (Moscow, 1982); for 1984, *Sbornik stat. materialov, 1985* (Moscow, 1986). See also: for 1940–1969, *Vestnik statistiki* 2 (1969): 92; for 1970–1974, *Zhenshchiny v SSSR* (Moscow, 1975), pp. 97, 100; for divorces in 1966, *Zhurnalist* 1 (January 1974), pp. 72–73. The number of divorces per 1,000 marriages was reported to be as high as 408 in 11 major cities in 1973, reaching 425 in Leningrad and 436 in Moscow; Perevedentsev, *Literaturnaia gazeta* 18 (April 30, 1975); for the U.S., *San Francisco Chronicle*, February 9, 1977, p. 1. In the U.S. in 1974 there were a total of 2,233,000 marriages and 948,000 divorces, and a marriage rate of 10.5 per 1,000 population. Recent Soviet figures are found in *Vestnik statistiki* 12 (1975), pp. 89–90, and 11 (1976), pp. 88–89.

Table 4

Population Size, Marriages, and Divorces, 29 Republic Capitals and Cities with over One Million Inhabitants, 1984

	Population size, in thousands	Number of marriages	Number of divorces	D/M (%)
Alma-Ata	1,068	11,415	5,544	48
Ashkhabad	356	3,458	1,519	44
Baku[1]	1,693	15,566	3,912	25
Vilnius	544	6,272	2,043	33
Gor'kii	1,399	12,254	5,315	43
Dnepropetrovsk	1,153	10,932	5,700	52
Donetsk	1,073	10,055	5,717	57
Dushanbe	552	5,204	2,259	43
Erevan	1,133	10,840	2,041	19
Kazan'	1,047	9,206	4,555	49
Kiev	2,448	23,312	12,314	53
Kishinev	624	6,868	3,002	44
Kuibyshev	1,257	12,097	6,565	54
Leningrad[1]	4,867	54,930	27,306	50
Minsk	1,472	13,659	6,144	45
Moscow[1]	8,642	86,536	44,554	51
Novosibirsk	1,393	14,914	7,759	52
Odessa	1,126	10,560	6,254	59
Omsk	1,108	12,254	5,993	49
Perm'	1,056	9,776	3,933	40
Riga	883	8,937	4,917	55
Sverdlovsk	1,300	12,666	5,586	44
Tallin	464	5,013	2,542	51
Tashkent	2,030	20,104	6,807	34
Tbilisi	1,158	10,182	3,064	30
Ufa	1,064	8,728	3,957	45
Frunze	604	5,970	2,170	36
Khar'kov	1,554	14,965	7,798	52
Cheliabinsk	1,096	10,732	5,035	47

1. Includes areas under the jurisdiction of the city soviet.

Source: Tsentral'noe Statisticheskoe Upravlenie SSSR, *Sbornik statisticheskikh materialov (v pomoshch' agitatoru i propagandistu)*, 1985 (Moscow: Finansy i statistika, 1986) pp. 180–81.

Table 5. The large number of divorces, and the fact that the over-whelming majority of the Soviet population is married, is indicative of the fact that people marry again (and perhaps again) after divorce. Taking 1984, for instance, we note that in that year 2,634,100 couples tied the knot. This was a first marriage for 2,127,200 of the men and 2,146,000 of the women. It thus was not a first marriage for about 20 percent of those getting married. As expected, as the age at marriage increases, the percentage of first marriages goes down. Thus in the age cohort marrying between 30 and 34 more than half of the men were not marrying for the first time. For the women it was close to 60 percent (reflecting the fact that women tend to marry at an earlier age).

One of the important consequences of this situation, as Pereveden-tsev has pointed out, and as can be deduced from the available data, is that there are about one million youngsters who are left without a (biological) father every year, since in practically all cases it is the mother who keeps the child (or children). Whether or not the mother remarries, the impact of divorce on the child is likely to be unsettling. Time and again, Soviet sources point out that the majority of children who are in trouble, either at school or "on the street," come from families that are themselves in trouble. Divorce is usually preceded by a period of family instability (often caused and compounded by alcohol-ism). After the divorce, inadequate supervision by an overworked and harried mother only exacerbates the problems of the children. The existence of this steady annual addition of about one million potentially troubled and troublesome youngsters is not the best omen for the production of a well-disciplined, hard-working, devoted Soviet citi-zenry in the years to come.

The implications of these statistics worry Soviet officials and ideo-logues. One concern most often expressed is fear about the young boys who are raised in an overwhelmingly female atmosphere (at home and in daycare centers). Another concern, not so often noted but deplored, is for the "masculinization" of girls who, in an atmosphere of equality of the sexes, often take on the less desirable attributes of their male comrades (fighting, delinquency, swearing, smoking, drinking, and so on). *Komsomol'skaia pravda* commented in 1985 on the increased fighting among girls, and female gangs, and linked these to the chang-ing interests of women, adding that "Women today are mastering male professions, breaking men's records, and taking new positions in the family. They are required to display completely new qualities in order to keep up with the pace of modern life."[7] The blurring of sex roles, at

Table 5

Number of Registered Divorces, by Length of Marriage and Age of Husband and Wife, USSR, 1984, in Thousands

| | Regis-tered divorces (total) | less than 1 year | Length of marriage | | | | | |
			1–2	3–4	5–9	10–19	20+	not known
Total	932.3	28.6	145.6	165.3	276.1	210.1	105.1	1.5
Including age less than 20								
Men	1.2	0.4	0.8	—	—	—	—	0.0
Women	12.5	3.3	8.4	0.8	—	—	—	0.0
20–24								
Men	110.5	10.3	55.1	35.8	9.2	—	—	0.1
Women	194.8	10.9	71.4	77.9	34.3	—	—	0.3
25–29								
Men	250.5	7.1	46.0	79.7	112.7	4.6	—	0.4
Women	242.0	5.6	31.3	49.6	138.0	17.2	—	0.3
30–34								
Men	201.6	3.8	18.6	25.0	94.9	59.1	—	0.2
Women	173.6	3.2	14.7	17.6	58.9	79.0	—	0.2
35–39								
Men	119.9	2.1	8.6	9.8	27.5	70.0	1.8	0.2
Women	102.9	1.6	6.9	7.5	20.3	62.1	4.4	0.1
40–44								
Men	77.6	1.2	4.6	4.7	11.5	40.9	14.5	0.2
Women	67.0	1.0	3.6	3.7	9.1	25.1	24.4	0.1
45–49								
Men	76.2	1.1	4.3	4.0	8.9	21.4	36.3	0.2
Women	64.1	0.9	3.5	3.4	6.8	15.3	34.0	0.2
50–54								
Men	38.2	0.6	2.2	1.9	3.9	6.2	23.3	0.1
Women	31.2	0.6	2.0	1.6	3.4	5.1	18.4	0.1
55–59								
Men	27.2	0.6	1.7	1.5	2.8	3.5	17.0	0.1
Women	24.1	0.6	1.6	1.3	2.4	3.3	14.8	0.1
60+								
Men	22.3	1.2	2.8	1.7	2.5	2.6	11.4	0.1
Women	15.6	0.8	1.7	1.1	1.6	1.9	8.5	0.0
Age unknown								
Men	7.1	0.2	0.9	1.2	2.2	1.8	0.8	0.0
Women	4.5	0.1	0.5	0.8	1.3	1.1	0.6	0.1

Source: Sbornik statisticheskikh materialov, 1985. p. 178.

least partly as a result of the decrease in intact families and clear role models for both girls and boys, is a matter of frequent comment in the media, in letters to the editor, and in articles. In addition, of course, the high and increasing rate of divorce has a negative impact on the birth-rate and the reproduction of the population. There is thus a seamless sequence of causality: the difficult situation brought about by massive and rapid urbanization leads to the break-up of a large number of families, which especially affects the children, who then go on to produce more problems.

We have mentioned that alcoholism has been an important element in causing families to break up, and one can easily understand the importance that the Gorbachev leadership has placed on trying to re-duce the impact of alcohol abuse on the entire society. We do have a detailed list of reasons for divorce in 637 cases in Western Belorussia for the years 1972–73, according to information given by each of the spouses and the opinion of the judges trying the cases. Alcoholism leads the list of reasons for both wives and judges, but not for the husbands, who give "incompatibility" twice as often as alcoholism as the reason. Other reasons such as infidelity, casual marriage, etc., can be examined in Table 6.

Family instability is, as one might expect, the end result of a multi-plicity of forces, alcoholism being only one of them. Another important factor, and one that receives increased attention and concern, is the sexual revolution that seems to be sweeping over the Soviet younger generations, and which is, the world over, attributed to the social disorganization and family instability characteristic of urban life. There is, for example, the increasingly greater acceptance of extra- or premarital sex, an element that is held to weaken the marriage relation-ship in general, but also leads to an increase in the rate of illegitimacy. There are scattered reports from many areas in the Soviet Union indi-cating a rise in illegitimate births and in the number of children con-ceived before marriage. Data on women giving birth to illegitimate children in Belorussia for the years 1959 and 1970 show that for every age category there was a significant increase in that eleven-year period, as can be seen from Table 7, below. Although the increases were considerable, the 98.1/1,000 births for women in the age brackets 25–29 in 1970 (about 10 percent) does not seem excessive, particularly when compared with similar figures in the West. In Perm' in 1966 it was found that 68 percent of the pregnancies among 15–19-year-olds be-gan before marriage, and 24 percent of the births in that group were to

Table 6

Reasons for Divorce in the Opinion of Husband, Wife, and Judge, Grodno Province, Western Belorussia, 1972–73 (637 divorce cases), Percent

| | According to the opinion of | | |
	Judge	Wife	Husband
Alcoholism	38.7	44.3	10.6
Incompatibility	15.1	6.7	22.2
Infidelity	9.4	12.6	15.3
Casual marriage	8.5	2.0	4.5
Long separation (owing to circumstances)	5.4	3.8	3.1
Loss of feeling for unknown reasons	5.3	8.6	12.3
Cruelty	3.6	5.6	0.6
Sentencing to deprivation of freedom for three or more years	3.3	2.6	2.1
Physical and mental illness	2.1	1.7	2.6
Interference of parents and relatives	1.5	4.4	11.3
Infertility	0.8	0.7	1.0
Physiological mismatch	0.3	0.3	0.5
Other reasons	6.0	6.7	6.0

Source: V. T. Kolokol'nikov, "Brachno-semeinie otnosheniia v srede kolkhoznogo krest'-ianstva," *Sotsiologicheskie issledovaniia*, no. 3 (1976), p. 82.

single women.[8] In 1985 Perevedentsev, citing another study of pregnancies in Perm', reported that of 1,000 pregnancies in that city, 317 mothers had a child 9 months or more after marriage; 271 mothers had a child during the first months of marriage; 140 mothers bore a child out of wedlock; and 270 women terminated the pregnancy by choice.[9] In Leningrad a study of firstborn babies registered in December and conceived before marriage showed a rise from 24 percent in 1963 to 38 percent in 1978.

While the official Soviet attitude is to deplore illegitimate births, its major concern in this respect seems to be those that take place among younger women, who are more likely to abandon their illegitimate children, and whose babies are more likely to be of low birth weight, premature, and thus more at risk, contributing to the infant mortality which is a major problem in the USSR nowadays (the Soviet infant mortality rate is almost three times higher than that in the United States). On the other hand, in the case of older women, who are emotionally and physically more mature, having children out of wed-

Table 7

Illegitimate Births per Thousand Unmarried Women, Belorussia, 1959 and 1970

Age group	1959	1970
15–19	2.7	7.1
20–24	16.3	73.9
25–29	36.8	98.1
30–34	39.1	87.2
35–39	27.1	47.2

Source: Larisa Kuznetsova, "Obeshchal zhenit'sia," *Literaturnaia gazeta*, April 14, 1973, p. 12.

lock tends to receive guarded endorsement. An article published in 1980, for example, argues that unmarried women who cannot marry because there are not enough eligible men should be encouraged to have children, while abortions should be discouraged or criticized.[10] Nonetheless, there is evidence that a great deal of stigma attaches to unmarried mothers, as shown, for example, in one letter to *Literaturnaia gazeta* from an unmarried woman who complained of ostracism directed not only against her but also against her child by the parents of her son's playmates. She also adds that generally speaking, children of unmarried mothers are not considered as suitable marriage partners.[11] Other articles in the media, especially in *Literaturnaia gazeta*, discuss the fact that there are many more women than men of marriageable age, and at least one suggests that the answer may be extramarital ties:

> I propose that we . . . recognize that along with . . . the quite stable expanse of the family, there exists a smaller but much more tempestuous sea of instability. . . . [W]e cannot eliminate it, the statistics stand in the way . . . we cannot marry 170 "brides" to 100 "grooms." . . . Life has its own intuition. To help the lonely is a very noble goal. But there is a minimum goal: not to interfere.[12]

Incidentally, the statistics used by the writer came from the 1970 census, which showed that for every 170 unmarried women between 18 and 42 there were only 100 eligible bachelors—i.e., unmarried men between 21 and 46.[13]

All these are major problems, and a source of great controversy and discussion in the Soviet Union. The falling birthrate, in particular, is a source of concern because of its implications for economic, political, and military developments. It raises the specter of depopulation. Some measures have been adopted in the past two decades to increase fertility and to provide support for children of low-income families.[14] Many advocate improvements in housing, household appliances, more flexible work hours for women, more daycare centers, and other similar steps. At the same time, as we have said, while there is an absolute need to increase the number of births in the Slavic areas to ensure replacement rates, the opposite need exists in the Southern Tier. As one Soviet demographer put it, the question is whether demographic policy should vary from region to region. Assuming that for the country as a whole a reproduction rate of 1.0–1.2 is optimally desirable,

> it is necessary to stimulate by various measures the birth of the first, second, and third child in the family . . . but beginning with the fourth child all measures of an encouraging nature should cease, or at a minimum significantly weaken. Such a system might stimulate fertility in areas where it is low and at the same time further the lowering of fertility where it is very high.[15]

The future of the Soviet family

The debate in the Soviet Union on the nature of the family, the manner in which it performs its educational and social functions, and what reforms are needed is lively, often brutally frank, and as public as it can be in the Soviet context. It appears to mobilize a great deal of interest, if not emotion, because it goes to the heart of the kind of society people want, or would like, to live in. It embraces people's most important, emotionally and psychologically charged relationships (between spouses, between parents and children, and between grandparents and grandchildren). Finally, it is an issue that is relatively "safe" to discuss, air, and debate. While foreign policy, the personalities of national leaders, and the basic ideological tenets that provide legitimacy to the Soviet regime are not fit subjects for discussion, much less public debate, the family, relations between spouses, the problem of juvenile delinquency, the equality (or lack of equality) between male and female burdens, femininity and masculinity, the falling birthrate and rising divorce rate, the harmfulness of alcohol, and related topics are fairly constant subjects of interest and argument.[16]

In the face of the growing concern about the Soviet family and family instability, the lack of family counseling in the country is striking. There is no program for the training of family therapists. It was reported in 1985 that there was only one family counseling center in the Soviet Union, in Moscow, where people may seek help for their problems with their children and marital troubles.[17] There is evidence that the Moscow model is being examined and imitated (or adapted) elsewhere, for example, in the Baltic republics, Bashkiria, and in a number of cities of the Russian Federation. One Soviet demographer has proposed that officials should be responsible for the sociodemographic condition of the area under their jurisdiction, just as they are held responsible for the fulfillment of production assignments. Should the birthrate drop, or the divorce rate rise, then the official in charge should have to account for it as he must for the production of steel or livestock breeding.[18] This is a startling notion, but logically it is in line with Soviet ideas of social planning and management.

These conditions, and many others related to them, all conspire to place the Soviet family in a difficult and precarious position. As mentioned earlier, the cultural lag is such that new systems of values that would make the situation more bearable, if not acceptable or manageable, have not yet developed to the point of being effective on a national scale. Again, the impact of these conditions, singly and in combination, on the socialization process of infants and children, and on the ability of the Soviet family to provide a comfortable and secure harbor for adults as well as children, must be seen as a major issue for Soviet society, and one with serious implications for the future. The Soviet regime is not likely to move toward a policy of phasing out or discouraging family formation (far from it), but it is not sure precisely what policy to pursue, particularly in the light of its many other conflicting priorities and its shortage of economic resources. To the degree that no other social agency (except for agencies of extrafamilial socialization, which are of questionable efficiency) can perform the tasks of the family, it may be expected that the weakened, structurally unsupported (in comparison with the extended family), splintered, confused family will continue to pose problems for Soviet society. Yet, the alternative of providing support to the family, to strengthen it, entails a danger for the Soviet regime—the danger of "privatization," the creation of comfortable nests of individuals who may become indifferent to the interests of the state and the larger society. It seems reasonable to expect that the Soviet regime will attempt in its policies to maintain a delicate balance, reinforcing the family so that it can accomplish the tasks mandated to it by society, while keeping it from becoming too solidary or entrenched and thus resistant to the demands of the workplace, the collective, the system at large.

There is yet another issue related to the family that is of some importance for the future functioning of Soviet society (or any other industrial society for that matter). These societies tend to be stratified, and the unit of each stratum or class is not so much the individual as the family or the household, whose members are treated as a solidary entity. The children of every household inherit the privileges and the disabilities of their parents' class position. In such a society, it is thus structurally impossible to provide full equality of opportunity to children unless they are removed from the family's orbit at a very young age. (This is not usually considered a feasible solution, as it may lead to a whole new series of serious problems resulting from the institutional upbringing of children.) The solidification of class stratification in the Soviet Union may already be a problem for the new leadership, which is seeking to implement social change in the face of entrenched class-interest groups, and which, to fulfill its ambitious development plans, must be able to tap potential talent and leadership ability wherever it may be found. This is both an ideological and to some degree a functional problem; but a radical solution could, in the long run, be more destructive than constructive.

It can be tempting, when one looks at contemporary trends, to predict the demise of the family. And yet, history has shown the family's resilience. It has changed, it has shrunk in size, and it has abandoned many of its former functions, yet it remains an all but indispensable institution for any society. It plays a crucial role in a multiplicity of critical social processes, from the net reproduction to the determining of the emotional stability and basic competence and character of the population, the activities of its juveniles, and the fate of the elderly. It may safely be predicted that the nature and the role of the family will continue to be the object of intense concern, scrutiny, and soul-searching in the Soviet Union. The interventionist proclivities of the Soviet leadership should lead us to expect a constant stream of studies, discussions, and eventually laws, resolutions, decrees, and regulations concerning the family, many of which may produce results unintended by those who craft them. But then, the unanticipated and surprising consequences of planned social action are one of the constant and intriguing features of Soviet society.

Notes

1. The translation of this quotation is taken from Anthony Olcott's essay, "*Glasnost*' and Soviet Culture," below.
2. Mydans 1985, 14.
3. Lapidus 1978, 233.
4. Mydans.
5. "Population . . . ," 6–7.
6. Lapidus, 239.
7. Ganelin 1985, 2.
8. Kon 1982.
9. "Authority's Opinion . . . ," 2.
10. Urlanis 1980, 16.
11. "Letter . . . ," 12.
12. Zhukovitskii 1984, 12.
13. Perevedentsev 1977, 13.
14. McAuley 1979.
15. Kvasha 1974.
16. Dimitrieva 1985, 2.
17. Mikhitarian 1985, 4.
18. Bednyi 1984, 6.

Bibliography

"Authority's Opinion: The First Child." 1985. *Komsomol'skaia pravda*, 26 April, 2. For an English translation see: *Current Digest of the Soviet Press* (hereafter, *CDSP*) 37(17): 20.

Bednyi, M. 1984. "Problems and Opinions: The Family and Demography." *Pravda*, 3 December. *CDSP* 36(49): 6.

Chislennost' i sostav naseleniia SSSR: Po dannym Vsesoiuznoi perepisi naseleniia 1979 goda. 1984. Moscow: Finansy i statistika.

Dmitrieva, C. 1985. "Make Sobriety the Norm: The Wineglass versus Childhood." *Komsomol'skaia pravda*, 8 June, 2. *CDSP* 37(23): 12.

Engels, F. 1884. *The Origin of the Family, Private Property, and the State*. New York, 1942.

Field, Mark G. 1956. "The Relegalization of Abortion in Soviet Russia." *New England Journal of Medicine* 255 (August): 421–27.

Field, Mark G., and David E. Anderson. 1969. "The Family and Social Problems." In *Prospects for Soviet Society*, edited by Allen Kassof. New York: Praeger, 386–417.

Ganelin, A. 1985. "Tomboys." *Komsomol'skaia pravda*, 5 July, 2. *CDSP* 37(29): 15.

Ivanova, V. 1983. "A Sociologist Studies the Problem: The Only Child." *Sovetskaia Rossiia*, 20 November, 3. *CDSP* 36(3): 15.

Juviler, Peter H. 1967. "Family Reform on the Road to Communism." In *Soviet Policy-Making*, edited by Peter H. Juviler and Henry W. Morton. New York: Praeger, 29–60.

———. 1980. "The Soviet Family in Post-Stalin Perspective." In *The Soviet Union Since Stalin*, edited by S. F. Cohen, A. Rabinowitch, and R. Sharlet. Bloomington: Indiana University Press, 227–51.

Kiltunen, A. 1985. "Danger: Home of Our Hopes." *Komsomol'skaia pravda*. *CDSP* 37(12): 3.

Kon, Iu. S. 1982. "On the Sociological Interpretation of Sexual Behavior." *Sotsiologicheskie issledovaniia* (2): 113–22. *CDSP* 34(24): 13.

Konovalov, O. E. 1985. "Medical and Demographic Aspects of the Illegitimate Birth Rate." *Sovetskoe zdravookhranenie* (7): 39–42. *CDSP* 37(39): 11.

Kvasha, A. Ia. 1974. *Problemy ekonomiko-demograficheskogo razvitiia SSSR*. Moscow: Statistika.

Lapidus, Gail Warshofsky. 1978. *Women in Soviet Society: Equality, Development, and Social Change*. Berkeley: University of California Press.

"Letter to the Editor" 1977. *Literaturnaia gazeta*, 4 May, 12. *CDSP*, 29(18): 1.

McAuley, Alastair. 1979. *Economic Welfare in the Soviet Union: Poverty, Living Standards and Inequality*. Madison: University of Wisconsin Press.

Mikhitarian, A. 1985. "Take Someone Else's Pain." *Sotsialisticheskaia industriia*, 30 March, 4. *CDSP*, 37(28): 16.

Mydans, Seth. 1985. "Social Revolution Sweeps through Soviet Home." *New York Times*, 25 August, 14.

Perevedentsev, V. 1977. "Bachelor Cities." *Literaturnaia gazeta*, 16 February, 13 . *CDSP*, 29(7): 16.

Podrastaiushchee pokoleniie. Demograficheskii aspekt. 1981. Moscow: Finansy i statistika.

"The Population of the Soviet Union." 1986. *Ekonomicheskaia gazeta* (43) (October): 6–7.

Sovetskaia molodezh'. Demograficheskii aspekt. 1981. Moscow: Finansy i statistika.

Tsentral'noe statisticheskoe upravlenie SSSR. 1982. *Sbornik statisticheskikh materialov, 1981*. Moscow: Finansy i statistika.

Tsentral'noe statisticheskoe upravlenie SSSR. 1986. *Sbornik statisticheskikh materialov 1985*. Moscow: Finansy i statistika.

Urlanis, Boris. 1980. "A Wanted Child." *Nedelia*, 1–7 December, 16. *CDSP* 32(49): 10.

Vasil'eva, E. K. 1975. *Sem'ia i ee funktsiia*. Moscow: Statistika.

Vorozheikin, E. M. 1973. *Brak i sem'ia v SSSR*. Moscow.

Zhukovitskii, Leonid. 1984. "A Writer's Notes: Where Have All the Real Men Gone?" *Literaturnaia gazeta*, 10 October 1984, 12. *CDSP* 37(5): 1.

LABOR PROBLEMS AND THE PROSPECTS FOR ACCELERATED ECONOMIC GROWTH

Vladimir Kontorovich

Gorbachev's economic objectives

Mikhail Gorbachev's main goals for the Soviet economy are to accelerate growth, improve the quality of output, and modernize the obsolete production apparatus. If these goals are to be achieved, it is essential that the economy have sufficient workers, with appropriate skill and education, assigned to the right jobs and motivated to perform their tasks well. In fact, there are problems with each of these aspects of labor—problems that have endured for some time and are responsible for the present alarming state of the Soviet economy, which Gorbachev vows to improve. His predecessors attempted to solve most of these problems without success.

This paper attempts to gauge Gorbachev's chances for success in solving the labor force problems that impede progress toward his overall economic goals. In addition, we examine what the policies already adopted[1] tell us about Gorbachev's general outlook (his preferences with regard to market and command instruments, inclination to continue or to break past patterns, take unpopular and ideologically impure measures). The first question informs us about the short-run course of the new leadership. The second question concerns the likely adjustments several years down the road. While the main focus of this paper is economic (policies are evaluated with respect to their contributions to the acceleration of growth), we will also note broader social implications of labor force policies.

Vladimir Kontorovich is president of Command Economies Research, Inc.

Let us begin by identifying specific problems of the labor force that are relevant to the goals of the new leader (the existence of most of these problems is well documented in both Soviet and Western literature). We classify problems of the labor force into two categories: those affecting the overall labor force, and those relating to particular groups, such as urban and rural workers, or specialists. The paper is divided into sections dealing with the problems of these groups. For each problem, we list conceivable policy options and the policies initiated or continued by the current leadership.

Each policy is evaluated on four dimensions: first, in terms of its probable effectiveness; second, with respect to its likely reception by workers themselves; third, with respect to its fit within the present command economic system; and finally, in terms of its origination. Most economic policies have a significant impact on the labor force. Policies in the areas of technological progress, investment, and agricultural production are no less important for solving labor force problems than policies directly addressing labor issues. This underscores the importance of our topic, but also makes it hard to deal with in a concise way. We will be able to evaluate some policies in much more detail than others.

General problems of the labor force

One of the main problems of the Soviet economy in the 1980s is slow growth of the labor force. This results from a slowdown in the growth of the able-bodied population under already high labor participation rates, a trend that is expected to persist into the 1990s.[2] Problems of labor force structure, motivation, and utilization can no longer be compensated by sheer numbers.

Almost all of the growth of the labor force comprises people of Muslim origin, who have on average lower skills than the rest of the population and are reluctant to migrate to labor-short regions.[3] Current policy is to send Muslim youths to vocational schools in Russian areas, in hopes that some of them will remain in these regions to work. So far, however, the numbers involved are insignificant.[4]

The health of the labor force has been deteriorating, along with that of the population as a whole.[5] More people are absent from work, and those who are present are becoming less productive. It is not clear what can be done about the health crisis, since its causes are not well understood. The anti-alcohol campaign may help. But massive reallocation of resources to the health care sector will probably also be needed.[6] Given the general tightness of investment and foreign currency in the twelfth five-year plan, such a reallocation is unlikely. The economic dimensions of the health crisis remain unclear. What is the cost imposed by the crisis on the economy? Has it contributed significantly to the slowdown of economic growth? How much would it cost to reverse declines in health?

All groups of labor—rural and urban workers, managers and specialists—are recruited from a common pool that is virtually devoid of growth, except in Muslim areas, and which also is in poorer health than before. These general problems exacerbate the shortage of workers.

The rest of this essay deals with the problems and policies specific to particular groups. Let us briefly review these problems. Rural labor problems are the most longstanding, being rooted in the devastation of the countryside under Stalin. By crippling agricultural production and the supply of food, problems of rural labor greatly aggravate already existing difficulties in the motivation of urban workers.

A second labor group, managers and officials, numbers only several hundred thousand, but these persons occupy positions of extreme importance. The major problem of this group—that of motivation—emerged in the 1970s, as a general unwillingness to punish officials led to deteriorating performance. The Andropov–Gorbachev discipline campaign is working to resolve this difficulty, as officials and managers are again being penalized for poor performance. The Soviet economy is now reaping the benefits of more energetic managers attempting to work more productively than before.[7] But managers have been an easy target, since they are a relatively small group of specially selected individuals in highly desired, privileged positions. Two other groups within the labor force, workers and specialists, do not possess these characteristics, and will be much more difficult to deal with.[8] The problems of these two groups must be addressed if long-run economic growth targets are to be taken seriously.

Excess supply of specialists

The problem

Specialists—graduates of higher or specialized secondary educational institutions—comprise almost a quarter of the total labor force in the Soviet Union.[9] The role of this group has increased as the society has developed, but at this time there are too many specialists in the Soviet economy. They are poorly trained and poorly paid, enjoy low prestige, and are largely unproductive. This means that money spent on their education and wages is wasted; that white-collar tasks are performed poorly and take too long to complete. The glut of specialists aggravates the shortage of workers, and the situation is worsening with time. The educational level of the different age cohorts varies significantly. As cohorts consisting mainly of relatively uneducated workers retire, new entrants are weighted toward persons with higher education.

Planners are alarmed by the disproportionate increase in the army of specialists with higher education relative to the rest of the labor force.[10] Although Soviet authors have been addressing this issue at least since the early 1970s, as have Western writers more recently, no real analysis of the problem has been produced.[11] It may be conjectured that the expansion of higher education was propelled by the inertia of the industrialization period, when there was a real deficit of specialists, and by a Yugoslav-style process in which every region pressed for its own university and polytechnical institute. As the pool of qualified teachers and students became exhausted, the quality of higher education declined. At the same time, the number of white-collar jobs expanded to absorb the new graduates. The mechanism of this expansion is not clear, but in the course of it the salaries of specialists were kept low. As a result, the pay of many groups of specialists fell below that of workers. The prestige of specialists has plummeted, partly as a result of the processes described above.

There is often not enough work for all specialists to do, so they are often assigned to routine tasks that do not require them to exercise their skills and knowledge. As a consequence, the morale of the specialists has declined over time. Many of them leave for better paying and more meaningful blue-collar jobs[12]; others pass their time at work unproductively.[13]

Overeducation may have contributed to the Soviet economic growth slowdown.[14] In theory, better-educated workers are more productive; as the number of man-hours worked by those who are better educated increases as a proportion of the whole, the productivity of labor also increases. But at any given time, the demand for workers with higher education is limited. If the educational level of workers increases in excess of the needs of the economy, the increase in labor quality will not result in higher growth.

Policies

The Gorbachev leadership has been especially active in reforming the labor market for specialists. The remuneration of researchers and designers in R&D institutions and industry is being restructured.[15] Salaries are becoming more graduated (five ranks of researchers instead of two); salaries of designers have been raised; heads of organizations are allowed to use savings in the planned wage fund to augment salaries of researchers and designers who work well, and they have been given more flexibility in establishing salaries of individual employees. Periodic certification of specialists is to be conducted. The stimulative role of bonuses will be increased.

The decree on salary restructuring incorporates some of the features of the Leningrad experiment. This experiment sought to apply such organizational innovations as the Shchekino system and the brigade, which originated in industry and construction, to engineering and design units.[16] In this experiment, salaries of employees who were made redundant were partially divided among the remaining workers, to compensate for higher work loads. Redundant specialists were transferred to blue-collar positions within the same institutions or found employment at other establishments. A somewhat different experiment, involving the salaries of managers in design and engineering units, is being conducted in Ul'ianovsk. It is expected that 6–10 percent of researchers and designers will be released in the course of the salary restructuring.[17]

Some of the least efficient R&D organizations are being closed, merged, or restructured, also generating staff redundancies.[18] Politburo member El'tsin, first secretary of the Moscow city party committee, stated that of 39 research institutes identified as "doing nothing for years," fifteen would be shut down. Thirty thousand science workers who did not pass regular evaluation would be transferred to production jobs.[19] Layoffs of R&D personnel and closings of entire institutions represent bold steps, and may serve later as a model for dealing with some of the problems of blue-collar workers. However, one should watch how widely these policies are applied, and also the final destination of the redundant specialists. The policy may be called successful if the closing of institutions is not restricted to a few well publicized instances, and if personnel released from R&D positions end up in blue-collar occupations where there is a shortage of workers. But there are serious obstacles to such transfers. Some of the new labor policies in the R&D sector may become mere rituals, while others may be detrimental to the quality of research and development performed.[20]

Researchers and designers, who are the focus of current policies, represent only a small part of all the specialists. Future policies will have to be much broader if the problem is to be solved. Reform of higher education, which is currently under preparation, is one such broad measure.[21] To deal with the overproduction of specialists at the source, admissions to institutions of higher education will have to be restricted. This has important social implications. Higher education has traditionally been a road to social mobility. In the past, education was expanding rapidly enough to accommodate ambitious young people, whatever their later disappointments. Now this avenue of social mobility has to be narrowed for the sake of further economic development.

Dealing with shortages of workers

It is argued sometimes that there is no shortage of workers in the Soviet economy since, by Western standards, factories are over-manned. True, with different institutional arrangements, fewer workers would be needed to produce the same output and the labor shortage would disappear. But this would be an altogether different economy. Given the prevailing degree of intensity of work and methods of its organization, there definitely is a deficit of workers in Soviet economy.

This shortage of workers has been steadily worsening since it first appeared in the early 1960s.[22] The underlying cause of the shortage is the insatiable demand of the enterprises for labor. Supply factors, such as the unwarranted expansion of higher education and of white-collar jobs and the recent decline in the rate of growth of the working-age population, have aggravated the situation. The direct impact of labor shortages on the economy is that there are not enough people to operate machines; thus capital is wasted. The indirect effect of labor shortages is to reduce the motivation of available workers. As enterprises compete to attract people, they are likely to relax their demands on performance.[23] Labor shortages make it impossible to institute a discipline campaign for workers as effective as that for managers. Excess demand for labor is one of the main causes of the deterioration of labor discipline, increasing incidence of absenteeism, and general decline in effort exerted at the workplace.[24] This, in turn, has been one of the major causes of the slowdown of economic growth, the main problem of the current leadership.

Cutting demand for workers

Labor shortages stem from inflated demand, and only by paring down demand can a durable solution of the problem be found. The physical basis of excess demand for labor is the continuing accumulation of excess workplaces—pieces of capital that require people to operate them.[25] One of the reasons for this is that machines are produced in large quantities without much technological improvement. Making a smaller number of more sophisticated and productive machines would result in accumulation of capital without adding new workplaces.[26] In this sense, policies for the acceleration of technological progress are also labor policies. Acceleration of technological progress is the philosopher's stone of the Soviet economy; if it can be accomplished, it will alleviate most economic problems. The acceleration of technological progress is central to Gorbachev's economic strategy, and involves a series of measures that are beyond the scope of this essay.

While too many machines are produced for some of the "main production processes," there is a lack of equipment for "auxiliary" processes (loading and unloading, intra-plant transportation, etc.). Reduction of manual labor through mechanization of these processes would release a large number of workers for other jobs. Comprehensive programs for cutting manual labor were adopted in the 1970s[27] and continue under Gorbachev, but their successes so far seem to be modest. One reason for very slow progress in such a seemingly straightforward task was the inertia and apathy of the Brezhnev era. Proliferation of "comprehensive programs," reflecting the multiplication of objectives and devaluation of the priority principle, is another, more fundamental cause. The new leadership has done away with the first cause of the slow progress of mechanization, but it is not clear how the other causes of this problem will be affected. The main feature of Gorbachev's plans—high growth rate targets—may well reinforce the traditional bias of both planners and managers in favor of "main production processes," which produce items that count toward plan fulfillment.[28] Mechanization of auxiliary processes would require an adjustment of the producers' output mix.

Reorienting investment from construction of new plants to reconstruction of existing plants was an objective of investment policy through the 1970s, but it was not achieved.[29] It remains one of the top priorities in investment policy, and, if successful, would alleviate labor shortages. Other intended benefits include shorter construction periods, and smaller expenditures on structures relative to equipment.

There are two kinds of obstacles to renovation. First, even where renovation of existing plants makes sense economically, all the economic actors (designers, construction and machinebuilding enterprises) still prefer building new plants, because of the incentives they are offered. These incentives (norms and prices in construction and design) can be changed. We should observe carefully whether the Soviet authorities, learning from the failures of reconstruction policy in the 1970s, have begun to change microeconomic incentives. Second, and more ominously, it may be the case that reconstruction rarely makes sense; that often the best solution would be to abandon old plants and build new ones. To find out whether this is the case, one should take a look at the actual, as opposed to estimated, costs of Soviet reconstruction projects, and also at the international practice in this area. It may be that the emphasis on reconstruction of existing plants is dictated more by social considerations than by economic efficiency, since reconstruction preserves part of the existing labor force of the enterprise. Alternatively, one would have to find jobs for the workers of the old plant and recruit new ones for a new plant, create housing and infrastructure around the new plant, etc.

Reconstruction lies at the heart of Soviet investment strategy, and is aimed at resolving problems of labor, technological progress, and construction. The efficiency of reconstruction, direct and indirect (taking into account worker mobility and infrastructure) merits further study.

Reduction in the number of excessive workplaces can be accomplished without acceleration of technological progress or reorienting production in the machinebuilding and construction sectors. It is necessary to retire obsolete and worn-out machines, which abound on factory floors, and transfer workers who operate these machines to work on newer machines in the second and third shifts.[30] Along with solving the problem of labor shortage, this would improve utilization of fixed capital, release floor space, and save repair costs of aged machinery (and release an army of repairmen). This policy was adopted not long before Gorbachev came to power under the name of "certification of workplaces."[31] The main difficulty with this policy is that it must be carried out by the enterprises, which are responsible for the accumulation of excess workplaces in the first place. There is also the problem of persuading workers to work late shifts. This policy has produced only very modest results so far.[32]

In the 1970s and early 1980s, planning of labor was more closely integrated with other aspects of planning at the national, sectoral, and regional levels, and labor targets played a more important role in enterprise plans. More measures along these lines are suggested in the Soviet economic literature.[33] However overburdened planners have been in the past, they did not have to worry much about labor input. Plans for investment and production were drawn up, and labor somehow appeared when and where it was needed. Now, the labor supply has to be planned deliberately, along with the other objects of planning—machines, materials, capacities, etc.

All of the policies described above have been embraced by Gorbachev. The scope of these policies is likely to be broadened, and it can be assumed that they will be pursued more energetically than in the past.[34] Party organs are told to emulate the experience of the Leningrad regional committee, which regulates investment and construction so as to cut labor demand. It is even suggested that any savings in the five-year investment quota of a region may be left at the disposal of regional authorities, giving them an incentive to economize on new construction.[35]

The targets of the twelfth five-year plan create new and unusual pressures on labor demand. In machinebuilding, both investment and retirement of equipment are to increase drastically. But if retirement of old equipment falls shorter of its target than investment does, as seems likely, the result will be increased worker shortages. It is therefore important to clarify the mechanism through which the new, higher retirement rates will be enforced. On the other hand, the twin pressures of labor shortage and high growth targets may force managers to retire obsolete machines and more fully utilize newer machines on their own initiative.

In the past, I evaluated the prospects of these policies negatively, suggesting that planners cannot handle many more new tasks, since they are already overburdened.[36] But it is possible that this problem may be given highest priority. Also, the distortions in the labor market now may be large enough for planners to deal with them in simple, if arbitrary, ways. For example, they might veto all designs for construction of production facilities that do not provide for a two- or three-shift operation; or impose arbitrary targets for the retirement of old equipment.

The policies that have been outlined here have the best chance of improving the labor situation (if any policy has). They are based on massive reallocation of resources by central command—something that has worked before in the Soviet economy. They are given high priority by a decisive new leadership.

Increasing the supply of workers

Policies aimed at increasing the supply of labor may bring only temporary relief to the shortage, because demand will undoubtedly expand further. With rates of labor force participation of the working-age population already high, there is not much that can be done to increase the supply of workers. Guest workers are utilized in extractive sectors and construction on a small scale. Their use is unlikely to expand sufficiently to significantly relieve the labor shortage.

Further solutions include expanding work by retirees (already undertaken under Brezhnev), and lengthening the work week (a measure that would be highly unpopular and possibly counterproductive).[37] Redundant white-collar workers are a potential new source of factory workers in the Gorbachev regime.[38]

School reform, which was initiated under Chernenko and has continued under the current leadership, aims at augmenting the labor force by allowing earlier entry and employing high school students in production jobs.[39] Another goal of the reform is to direct more entrants toward blue-collar jobs.

Another policy currently being implemented aims at increasing the labor supply by ferreting out the few remaining individuals who are not holding state jobs and putting them to work, and by shortening the intervals between jobs or between school and work. Labeled the Novopolotsk system, after the town in which it was first implemented, this system is now used in all of Belorussia, and in some localities in other republics.[40] The system monitors individual mobility within a given locality and enforces laws already on the books against those who do not hold state jobs. Local employment bureaus take censuses of the unemployed able-bodied population and also collect data from enterprises, schools, and police on individuals who have been fired or have resigned, graduated from schools, or moved into the locality. These individuals are then offered jobs. ''Prophylactic and educational measures'' are taken for those who remain out of work for a long time. This policy will not increase the labor supply significantly, because there are too few employable persons without jobs. In Belorussia this system deals with ''tens of thousands.''[41] But the Novopolotsk system's monitoring program, coupled with coercive laws, may be used in many other ways. It is already being used to enforce the ''unearned income'' decree.[42] It is also an effective means for restricting labor mobility, thus mitigating the effects of shortages of workers on labor discipline.

Motivating workers to work better

There are three kinds of problems with respect to the motivation of Soviet workers. Two problems (and the policies developed to solve them) are to a large degree specific to the Soviet economy. These are the low effectiveness of disciplinary measures, given the shortage of workers, and the equally low effectiveness of monetary remuneration, given the shortage of consumer goods. The third problem, that of a gap between rewards and individual effort, is common to the management of large hierarchical organizations everywhere.

Restoring the effectiveness of disciplinary measures

Since workers can evade disciplinary measures by changing jobs, managers are reluctant to tighten discipline for fear of losing them. One way to make workers sensitive to disciplinary measures is to restrict worker mobility among jobs, partially reinstituting pre-1956 arrangements. This move would do away with the sellers' market for labor by eliminating the market mechanism itself.

There is constant discussion about the need to take measures against excess labor mobility, to make frequent job-hopping costlier for workers. One step in this direction was taken a few years ago, when the practice of changing jobs twice in a year was decreed to be an interruption of one's work record, with detrimental consequences for retirement benefits.[43]

Further barriers to labor mobility were erected by a decree of August 1983 which allowed managers to demote employees for up to three months; employees cannot resign during this period.[44] Workers resigning ''without valid causes'' have to give two months' notice; one's work record remains uninterrupted only if new employment is found within three weeks after leaving a job. Workers fired for lack of discipline will have their bonuses at the new jobs halved for the first three months. Advertising of vacancies at the enterprises must be channeled through local employment agencies. The decree also institutes additional sanctions for infractions of labor discipline.

These decrees, predating Gorbachev, have not solved the problem of worker discipline. The topic of discipline remains prominent in the new leader's pronouncements. Attempts to restrict labor mobility continue.

The Novopolotsk system, mentioned above, is potentially a way of restricting the labor market. Under this system, all hirings in a given locality are directed through the local employment office, giving it the power of a monopsonist. Since one of the tasks of the system is to combat job-hopping, the office may wield its power to restrict the freedom to change jobs. The system is still in the early stages of development and it is not clear how effective it will be. Obviously, the information-processing requirements of tracking the mobility of individual workers are immense and may overwhelm the capacities of the employment bureaus. Enterprise managers starved for labor may well hire workers directly, rather than through the bureau. On the other hand, given the involvement of the Ministry of Internal Affairs (i.e., the police), there is a good deal of force behind this policy. It is based on allocation of a resource by command, which is the defining principle of the Soviet economy, and the kind of thing the Soviet authorities know how to do.

Making monetary rewards more attractive to workers

Just as the shortage of workers makes punishment ineffective, so the shortage of consumer goods weakens the effectiveness of monetary rewards. An extra ruble of remuneration elicits less effort, if it must be channeled into forced savings, than it would if it could contribute to the acquisition of long-coveted consumer goods.

Balance in the consumer goods market can be achieved either by cutting effective demand or by increasing supply. The first option means cutting cash balances in the hands of the population through a currency reform.[45] This, of course, would be an extremely unpopular measure for those individuals who would lose money.[46] However, it may be quite popular with the ''have-nots,'' who are increasingly irritated by inequalities of wealth.[47] Such a policy would have to be adopted unexpectedly, so as to prevent panic buying of goods in state trade to use up currency. It is therefore futile to attempt to look for forewarnings of such a policy.

On the supply side, the consumer market may be balanced by increasing the volume and/or price of goods and services supplied by the state, or by allowing greater leeway to individual initiative. Investment in the state consumer goods sector will be *cut* in the current five-year plan.[48] The available resources will have to be used to better effect to increase the supply of consumer goods and services. Two recent major decrees were aimed at increasing supplies by improving planning and organization in agriculture and light industry. Retail trade is also being reformed.[49]

Gorbachev clearly hopes that agricultural performance will improve especially quickly in response to his reorganization,[50] but there are many indications that the reorganization of agriculture has been essentially cosmetic.[51] The impact of another recent decree, the Comprehensive Program for Development of Consumer Goods and Services Production in 1986–2000, will surely be even smaller than that of the decrees just mentioned.[52] Comprehensive programs are meant to overcome the segmentation and departmental bias in planning by sectoral ministries. But their impact in such areas as R&D and innovation, where they are widespread, has been weak. The consumer sector does not need better coordination of individual actors, which is what programs do. Rather, more resources, flexibility, and better incentives are needed.

It is difficult to increase the physical volume of salable consumer goods and services in the state sector. But the same effect can be gained at a stroke of a pen by raising prices. This would both soak the money from the population and correct the long-standing irrationalities wherein many food items are sold far below cost. Sentiment in favor of such a move was voiced by the first secretary of the Volgograd regional party committee at the Twenty-seventh Party Congress. The Gosagroprom decree contained provisions for raising retail prices for certain seasonal food products, and most recent evidence indicates that food prices in "cooperative" stores were indeed raised. Of course, food price increases in the state retail network may be even more unpopular than currency reform, for they will hurt all strata of the population.

Lifting restrictions on various forms of individual economic activity may help balance the consumer market without diverting resources from the state's goals. Some individuals will become better off than others, but nobody will be penalized, as they would with price increases or currency reform. The freeing of small-scale private initiative has worked in other socialist countries, and this is what many observers expect from Gorbachev. The press is brimming with proposals for expanded individual enterprise, as never before.[53] But official policy in this respect is timid and contradictory. Family contracting in agriculture was mentioned in Gorbachev's speech at the Twenty-seventh Party Congress, and later incorporated into the decree on Gosagroprom. Another potentially promising policy was the revival of cooperatives for the production of consumer goods and services.[54] The relative flexibility of this organizational form helped the cooperatives play a significant role in the immediate postwar years, before their abolition in the late 1950s.

But all this was rendered meaningless in May 1986 by the drastic decree on "unearned incomes."[55] This decree emptied collective farm markets in the middle of the summer, as police prevented shipments of produce and harassed sellers.[56] The official attitude toward private farm plots, the single largest type of individual enterprise, remains lukewarm.[57]

The unearned incomes decree can be viewed as a labor policy for the second economy. It seeks to bring regulation and remuneration of work in the second economy in line with the official economy. This destroys the very reason for the existence of the second economy. As long as the authorities insist that no one earn more than the official rates, and institute thorough checks and controls to insure this, no organizational innovation will make a difference.

In the fall of 1986 the mass media started to condemn the way the unearned incomes decree was being implemented.[58] Then, in a stunning policy reversal, a new law, seemingly favorable to individual economic activity, was adopted.[59] But true legitimation of private enterprise in the Soviet Union must be problematic, even with consistent support from the leadership, and policy zigzags such as observed in the course of 1986 discourage all but the most risk-loving entrepreneurs.

Enforcing discipline in the state sector without clamping down on the second economy would be inconsistent. Besides, such a clampdown would be popular with the majority of the population, who do not profit directly from private economic activity. The clampdown on "unearned incomes" may signal that Gorbachev cares deeply about the popularity of his policies. If so, the unpopular measures listed above have no chance of being adopted. The options in this area are either politically risky, or not very effective. So far, Gorbachev has pursued only policies falling in the latter group.

Forging closer links between pay and effort

As long as money does not lose its utility completely, linking workers' earnings to performance will benefit the economy. Soviet authorities are constantly tinkering with pay schemes for workers. The two incentive pay schemes that are currently being widely implemented are the establishment of brigades working under a single contract, and the Belorussian railroad experiment.

Brigades were widely propagated in the late 1970s and early 1980s. A brigade is a group of workers performing a set of technologically related operations. The novelty consists in paying the brigade as a whole, rather than individual workers, and tying pay to the volume of "final ouput" of the brigade. Remuneration is divided among workers by the brigade itself; ideally, the chief of the brigade is elected by its members, who also decide on membership. The enterprise administration is required to guarantee the brigade certain supplies of materials and use of machines.[60]

While some brigades are spectacularly successful, most differ from the usual organization of work in name only. Brigades do not make a difference in the performance of the sectors in which they are widespread.[61] Managers cannot guarantee supplies of materials to brigades, given the well-known problems with the supply system. Nor can managers guarantee the brigades constant use of necessary equipment without severely hampering their ability to maneuver resources so as to achieve enterprise targets.[62] In the absence of such guarantees, the establishment of brigades working under contract makes workers bear all the risks of the enterprise—supply uncertainty, plan changes, etc. Few workers should be expected to agree to these risks. Brigade organization goes against the letter and spirit of enterprise organization, which is rigidly hierarchical, with its "one boss" (edinonachalie) principle; the existing rules and regulations do not allow the flexibility needed for the brigade to operate. Finally, the brigade is not a universally applicable organizational form. It requires that the output of a brigade be well defined, observable, and separable from the outputs of other brigades. This is the case for some types of work in construction and agriculture—the sectors in which brigades originated. But in most types of enterprises, brigade organization either cannot be implemented or is inferior to hierarchical organization.[63] The most recent innovation seeks to organize the work of the whole enterprise along lines similar to the brigade system.[64] This is still in the "experimental" stage, but seems to be destined for wide-scale diffusion.

The Belorussian railroad experiment also incorporates some features of the celebrated Shchekino enterprise experiment[65]: workers are released and a portion of the wage fund, retained by the enterprise, is used to remunerate the remaining workers who shoulder the tasks of those released. The lessons of the Shchekino experiment, now about twenty years old, can be used to evaluate the effectiveness and the likely speed of diffusion of this new modification.

What Gorbachev's labor policies tell us about his general outlook

Practically every policy under way at the time of Gorbachev's ascent is being continued under his leadership, which suggests that he is a man of stability and continuity, despite constant claims of making a sharp break with the Brezhnev era. The much heralded celebration of the fiftieth anniversary of the Stakhanov movement in 1985 established continuity of Gorbachev's policies with the more distant past. Indeed, the old policies for cutting labor demand are being pursued with greater vigor. New policies have been adopted in the areas of consumer goods and services and with respect to white-collar labor, but it is probable that many of these policies were drafted before Gorbachev took office.

Most significant is the fact that most of the policies adopted or vigorously pressed by Gorbachev are based on central planning and commands. The two minor exceptions concern provision of consumer goods (where the command principle has long been relaxed) and establishment of brigades (which seems to be ritualistic). This supports the view of Gorbachev as basically conservative in terms of the content of his policies, though radical in terms of their implementation.[66]

This conclusion should perhaps be modified for the longer run. Gorbachev's economic (and political) agenda has been getting more radical since the 1986 Party Congress. If this process continues, more radical measures may also be expected in the area of labor policy.

The Gorbachev leadership has shown that it can crack down on managers and officials, researchers and designers, participants in the second economy, and those who drink excessively. There is some hint of getting tougher with workers (on issues other than alcohol) in the talk of price increases. But to date, no broadly unpopular policy has been adopted.

In a command economy, commands work better than other means. This suggests that Gorbachev's labor policies may have some success. Current policies concerning white-collar work may be effective, if pursued on a wider scale (though they may have some strong side effects). The success of policies concerning blue-collar labor is more doubtful, though some progress cannot be ruled out. In any case, the success of Gorbachev's labor policies will not mean a balancing of demand and supply for labor, or providing workers with strong incentives. The very nature of command economy breeds shortages. The Soviet economy (like any large hierarchical organization) has trouble providing high-powered incentives. These problems cannot be resolved within the confines of the current system; but this does not mean that they must continue mounting. The latter would be tantamount to predicting eventual collapse of the whole system under the weight of insoluble problems.

Command economy is a viable system. While it cannot solve its immanent problems, it can prevent them from getting out of hand, just as capitalist economy cannot solve the problems of unemployment and cyclical instability, but learns to cope with them. Such adjustments were not made in the past because of Brezhnev's self-satisfied, immobilist style. This leadership style has clearly changed. The current leadership cares enough to attack the most pressing problems, and to pressure the bureaucracy into implementing the new policies. Bureaucratic resistance has become risky for bureaucrats.

Alleviating today's worst problems by giving them high priority means that the priority of other problems must be downgraded. The authorities may be sowing the seeds of tomorrow's crisis while dealing with today's. Deep-seated problems can be alleviated only at a cost.

Notes

1. We will refer to all of the policies of the current leadership as "Gorbachev policies," although this may be a misleading characterization if the leadership is split on some policies.

2. See Rapawy and Baldwin 1983.

3. Feshbach 1983a; Eberstadt 1983, 191–2. A study of the Central Asian economy is currently being undertaken by Dr. Boris Rumer.

4. Latifi and Usanov 1984. This was also discusssed at the last party congress.

5. Davis and Feshbach (1980) and Eberstadt (1981) were the first to write on

the health crisis. See also Eberstadt 1983, 192–6; Feshbach 1983a; Rapawy and Baldwin 1983.

6. Davis 1983.

7. See Kontorovich 1985a.

8. *Ibid.*, 28–30.

9. There were 31 million specialists in the Soviet economy in 1982. See Ivanov 1984, 3.

10. Kostin 1984, 36–7.

11. Teague 1985, 27–28.

12. In ferrous metallurgy, 18% of all engineers occupy blue-collar positions. See Parfenov 1985.

13. A survey of specialists holding blue-collar jobs in the "Iuganskneftegaz" association, where there are 2,000 such specialists, indicated that the motives are both low pay in white-collar positions and the high share of nonprofessional, clerical tasks in such positions. See Byk 1986, 36–7.

14. Bergson (1983, 45) could not find overeducation in the Soviet economy because he was using U.S. data on productivity differentials among groups with different levels of education. He estimated that education contributed 0.37 percentage points to the average annual growth rate in 1950–60; 0.54 percentage point in 1960–70; and 0.47 percentage points in 1970–75. That is, an increase in the educational level of labor weakly counteracted the growth slowdown in the 1960s, and marginally contributed to it in the early 1970s.

Let us assume that education indeed contributed 0.54 percentage points to the average annual growth rate in the 1960s. Let us further assume that because of overeducation, increases in the educational level of labor ceased to contribute to growth after 1970. This would mean that overeducation accounts for more than 65% of the decline in Bergson's "unexplained residual" from the 1960s to the early 1970s, and for 34% of the decline in the growth rate of total factor productivity in the same period. Bergson (1983, 45) estimated that total factor productivity growth rate declined from 1.83% in the 1960s to 0.26% in 1970–75; his unexplained residual declined from 0.98% to 0.16%.

Of course, overeducation, if it did occur, could hardly be as abrupt and complete as we have assumed here; its impact on growth must be more evenly distributed over time and of smaller magnitude. This exercise is intended only to show that the impact of overeducation on growth is potentially significant, and is therefore worth studying.

15. "V TsK KPSS, Sovete Ministrov . . ." 1985.

16. See Nikitin 1986.

17. "Ne za stepen' . . ." 1986.

18. "Nauka: neizbezhnost' . . ." 1986.

19. El'tsin reportedly delivered this speech on April 11, 1986, in the House of Political Education in Moscow, to propagandists. A genuine-looking account of the speech was published in *Novoe Russkoe Slovo* (New York), 1 August 1986.

20. See, e. g., "Za stepen'—prosto . . ." 1986.

21. "Osnovnye napravleniia . . ." 1986.

22. Evidence is summarized in Kontorovich 1986, 184; details are presented in Kontorovich 1985, sections 9.4–9.7.

23. See Kontorovich 1987.

24. See Teague 1985, 4–5, 11–12. Alcoholism, a general problem in the labor force, has been another cause of deterioration of discipline.

25. See Kontorovich 1986, 183–4 on the historical trend. The trend continues; see "Perevooruzhat' . . ." 1986.

26. Kontorovich 1987.

27. Ministries are given targets for the reduction of manual labor. See Schroeder 1982, 15–16.

28. The idea that Gorbachev's insistence on impossibly high growth rates will elicit from economic actors the very behavior patterns which he set out to change has been voiced by Ed Hewett and Herbert Levine.

29. See Rumer 1984, chapter 2.

30. "Obsolete workplaces comprise one third of all workplaces in machinebuilding, assuming two-shift operation" ("Perevooruzhat' . . ." 1986).

31. "V Tsentral'nom . . ." 1984.

32. See Mironov 1986; "Mneniia, opyt, problemy" 1986; Prigarin 1986; Tikidzhiev 1986.

33. Cited in Schroeder 1982, 9; Kontorovich 1985, 9.10.2 and 9.10.3.

34. Gorbachev 1986.

35. *Ibid.*

36. Kontorovich 1985, 9.10.3.2.

37. See Schroeder 1982, 19–20, for an evaluation of these policies.

38. See also Goodman and Schleifer, 1983, pp. 327–330.

39. See *O reforme* . . . 1984, 6, 18, 39, 43, 51; and Malyshev 1986.

40. See Fomich 1985; Chevanin 1985; and Simurov 1986.

41. Simurov 1986.

42. *Ibid.*

43. See Teague 1985, 10.

44. "V TsK KPSS, Sovete Ministrov . . ." 1983.

45. See Birman 1983, 70–91, on currency reform.

46. The rumors of an impending cancellation of deposits in savings institutions have apparently been so persistent that *Pravda* published a denial by the chairman of Gosbank ("Garantirovano . . .").

47. Sentiments for levelling wealth have recently found their way into the press. See Lisichkin 1986; "Chitateli 'LG'. . ." 1986.

48. Noren 1986. It is reasonable to assume that allocation of foreign currency to the consumer goods sector also will not increase.

49. See the decrees on the creation of Gosagroprom (*Pravda*, 29 March 1986) and "On improvement of planning, incentives, and management of production of consumer goods in light industry" (*Pravda*, 6 May 1986). On retail trade see "V Politburo . . ." 19 July 1986.

50. Somov and Stepnov 1986; Platoshkin 1986; Strelianyi 1986, 240.

51. See "Sovetuias' . . ." 1986.

52. "Kompleksnaia . . ." 1985.

53. See, for example, Fomin 1986.

54. Kabalkin and Khinchuk 1986; Khinchuk 1986; Zhurkin 1986; "V Politburo . . ." August 16, 1986.

55. "O merakh . . ." 1986.

56. Brovkin and Gorbuntsov 1986; Bublichenko 1986.

57. Poliakov 1986.

58. See, e. g., Zhukhovitskii 1986.

59. "Zakon . . ." 1986.

60. Popov and Shcherbakov 1984.

61. *Ibid.* On ritualistic organizational innovations, see Kontorovich and Shlapentokh, section 2.4.

62. See Fomin 1984.

63. Williamson (1985, chapter 9) compares an arrangement similar to the brigade, "internal contracting," to hierarchical organization, and finds the latter

more efficient.

64. Called *kollektivnyi podriad*. See a series of articles under the common title "Vtoroe . . ." (1986).

65. See Rutland 1984 for analysis of the Shchekino experience.

66. See Rumer and Shlapentokh 1985 for a forecast of just such a course by Chernenko's successor. A similar evaluation of Gorbachev's outlook is in Gustafson and Mann 1986, 14–16.

References

Adam, Jan, ed. 1982. *Employment Policies in the Soviet Union and Eastern Europe.* London: Macmillan.

Bergson, Abram and Levine, Herbert S., eds. 1983. *The Soviet Economy—Towards the Year 2000.* London: George Allen and Unwin.

Bergson, Abram. 1983. "Technological Progress." In: Bergson, Levine.

Birman, Igor'. 1983. *Ekonomika nedostach.* New York: Chalidze Publications.

Brovkin, V., and Gorbuntsov, D. 1986. "Vinovat li ogurets?" *Pravda*, 14 July.

Bublichenko, M. 1986. "Peregnuli." *Pravda*, 4 August 4.

Byk, Iu. G. 1986. "Spetsialisty na rabochikh dolzhnostiakh?" *Ekonomika i organizatsiia promyshlennogo proizvodstva*, no. 5.

"Chitateli 'LG' o netrudovykh dokhodakh." 1986. *Literaturnaia gazeta*, 4 June.

Chevanin, V. 1985. "Samyi tsennyi kapital." *Pravda*, 12 August 12.

Davis, Christofer, and Feshbach, Murray. 1980. *Rising Infant Mortality in the USSR in the 1970s.* U.S. Bureau of the Census, Series P–95, no. 74 (September).

Eberstadt, Nick. 1981. "The Health Crisis in the USSR." *The New York Review of Books*, 19 February 19.

———. 1983. "Overview." In: U.S. Congress 1983.

Feshbach, Murray. 1983a. "Issues in Soviet Health Problems." In: U.S. Congress 1983.

———. 1983b. "Trends in the Soviet Muslim Population—Demographic Aspects." In: U.S. Congress 1983.

Fomich, A. 1985. "Poshli na rabotu." *Pravda*, 10 March 10.

Fomin, V. 1984. "Urozhai vsemu venets." *Literaturnaia gazeta*, 6 April.

———. 1986. "Riadom s izvozchikom." *Literaturnaia gazeta*, 23 July 23.

"Garantirovano gosudarstvom." 1986. *Pravda*, 19 February 19.

Goodman, Ann, and Schleifer, Geoffrey. 1983. "The Soviet Labor Market in the 1980s." In: U.S. Congress 1983.

Gorbachev, M. S. 1986. "O piatiletnem plane ekonomicheskogo i sotsial'nogo razvitiia SSSR na 1986–1990 gody i zadachakh partiinykh organizatsii po ego realizatsii." *Pravda*, 17 June.

Gustafson, Thane, and Mann, Dawn. 1986. "Gorbachev's First Year: Building Power and Authority." *Problems of Communism* (May-June).

Ivanov, A. P. 1984. *Opredelenie potrebnosti v spetsialistakh i zatrat na ikh podgotovku.* Leningrad: Leningrad University Press.

Kabalkin, A., and Khinchuk, V. 1986. "Obsluzhivaiet kooperativ." *Pravda*, 21 April.

Khinchuk, V. 1986. "Chto mogut kooperativy?" *Pravda*, 12 July 12.

"Kompleksnaia programma razvitiia proizvodstva tovarov narodnogo potrebleniia i sfery uslug na 1986–2000 gody." 1986. *Pravda*, 9 October 9.

Kontorovich, Vladimir. 1985a. "Productivity in the Soviet Economy." Report to the Director of Net Assessment, Office of the Secretary of Defense, Washington, D.C.: Foundation for Soviet Studies.

———. 1985b. "Discipline and Growth in the Soviet Economy." *Problems of Communism* (November-December).

————. 1986. "Soviet Growth Slowdown: Econometric vs. Direct Evidence." *American Economic Review Papers and Proceedings* 76(2) (May).

————. 1987. "Soviet Investment Process and Capital-Labor Substitution." In: John P. Hardt and Carl H. McMillan, eds., *Planned Economies: Confronting the Challenges of the 1980s.* New York: Cambridge University Press (forthcoming).

Kontorovich, Vladimir, and Shlapentokh, Vladimir. 1986. *Organizational Innovation: Hidden Reserve in the Soviet Economy.* The Carl Beck Papers in Russian and East European Studies, no. 507. University of Pittsburgh.

Kostin, L. 1984. "Rezervy ispol'zovaniia trudovykh resursov." *Ekonomika i organizatsiia promyshlennogo proizvodstva* (1).

Latifi, Otakhon, and Usanov, Vladimir. 1984. "Rabochee popolnenie." *Pravda*, June 18.

Lisichkin, Gennadii, 1986. "Blagotvoritel'nost' iz chuzhogo karmana." *Literaturnaia gazeta*, 19 February 19.

Malyshev, Iu.. 1986. "Rukami shkol'nikov." *Pravda*, 25 August.

Mironov, N. 1986. "Rabochee mesto." *Pravda*, 25 August.

"Mneniia, opyt, problemy." 1986. *Ekonomika i organizatsiia promyshlennogo proizvodstva* (4).

"Nauka: neizbezhnost' perestroiki." 1986. *Literaturnaia gazeta*, 4 June.

"Ne za stepen', a za trud." 1986. *Literaturnaia gazeta*, 15 January.

Nikitin, Aleksandr. 1986. "Inzhenernyi eksperiment." *Pravda*, 7 April.

Noren, James. 1986. "Soviet Investment Strategy under Gorbachev." paper presented at the annual meeting of the American Association for the Advancement of Slavic Studies, New Orleans, La. (November).

"O merakh po usileniiu bor'by s netrudovymi dokhodami." 1986. *Pravda*, 28 May.

O reforme obshcheobrazovatel'noi i professional'noi shkoly. 1984. Sbornik dokumentov i materialov. Moscow: Politizdat.

"Osnovnye napravleniia perestroiki vysshego i srednego spetsial'nogo obrazovaniia." 1986.*Pravda*, 1 June.

Parfenov, V. 1985. "Chelovecheskii faktor." *Pravda*, 20 May.

"Perevooruzhat' mashinostroenie." 1986. *Pravda*, 8 July.

Platoshkin, A. 1986. "Ne s kabinetov nachinaetsia." *Pravda*, 19 May.

Poliakov, V. 1986. "Domashnii tsekh." *Pravda*, 21 July.

Popov, G., and Shcherbakov, V. 1986. "Dialektika podriada." *Pravda*, 27 June.

Prigarin, A. A. 1986. "'General'naia uborka' v masshtabakh otraslei: kak my k nei gotovy." *Ekonomika i organizatsiia promyshlennogo proizvodstva* (4).

Psacharopoulos, G. 1984. "The Contribution of Education to Economic Growth: International Comparisons." In: Kendrick, John W., ed., *International Comparisons of Productivity and Causes of Slowdown.* Cambridge, Ma.: Ballinger.

Rapawy, Stephen, and Baldwin, Godfrey. 1983. "Demographic Trends in the Soviet Union: 1950–2000." In: U.S. Congress 1983.

Rumer, Boris Z. 1984. *Investment and Reindustrialization in the Soviet Economy.* Boulder, Colorado: Westview.

Rumer, Boris, and Shlapentokh, Vladimir. 1985. "Will Soviets Follow China, or Return to Stalinomics?" *The Christian Science Monitor*, 7 February, 9.

Rutland, Peter. 1984. "The Shchekino Method and the Struggle to Raise Labour Productivity in Soviet Industry." *Soviet Studies* 36(3) (July).

Schroeder, Gertrude E. 1982. "Managing Labor Shortages in the Soviet Union." In: Adam 1982.

Simurov, A. 1986. "Chelovek i rabota." *Pravda*, 8 August.

Somov, V., and Stepnov, V. 1986. "Illiuziia uskoreniia." *Pravda*, 18 May.

"Sovetuias' s narodom." 1986. *Pravda*, 31 July.

Strelianyi. Anatolii. 1986. "Raionnye budni." *Novyi mir* (1).

Teague, Elizabeth. 1985. "Labor Discipline and Legislation in the USSR: 1979–85." *Radio Liberty Research Bulletin*, 16 October.

Tikidzhiev, R. N. 1986. "Rabochie mesta, trudovye resursy i kapital 'nye vlozheniia." *Ekonomika i organizatsiia promyshlennogo proizvodstva* (4).

U.S. Congress. 1983. Joint Economic Committee, *Soviet Economy in the 1980's: Problems and Prospects*. Part II. Washington, DC: Government Printing Office.

Williamson, Oliver E. 1985. *The Economic Institutions of Capitalism*. New York: Free Press.

"V Politburo TsK KPSS." 1986. *Pravda*, 19 July.

"V Politburo TsK KPSS." 1986. *Pravda*, 16 August.

"V Tsentral 'nom Komitete KPSS." 1984. *Pravda*, 13 November.

"V TsK KPSS, Sovete Ministrov SSSR i VTsSPS." 1983. *Ekonomicheskaia gazeta* (33) (August), 4.

"V TsK KPSS, Sovete Ministrov SSSR i VTsSPS." 1985. *Ekonomicheskaia gazeta* (29) (July).

"Vtoroe dykhanie podriada." 1986. *Ekonomika i organizatsiia promyshlennogo proizvodstva* (1).

"Zakon SSSR 'Ob individual 'noi trudovoi deiatel 'nosti.'" 1986. *Pravda*, 21 November.

"Za stepen'-prosto, za trud slozhno." 1986. *Literaturnaia gazeta*, 14 May.

Zhukhovitskii, Leonid. 1986. "Anatomiia peregiba." *Literaturnaia gazeta*, 15 October.

Zhurkin, N. 1986. "Pervye prikidki." *Pravda*, 24 May.

A NOBLE EXPERIMENT?
GORBACHEV'S ANTIDRINKING CAMPAIGN

Vladimir G. Treml

The campaign

Gorbachev's antidrinking campaign[1] was launched in May 1985 with announcements of numerous far-reaching measures designed to reduce drinking and alcohol abuse.[2] Among the most important measures were the raising of the minimum drinking age to 21, restriction of the hours of sale of alcoholic beverages to 2–7 p.m. and reduction of the number of stores and restaurants selling or serving alcohol. The penalties for being drunk in public, drinking or being intoxicated during working hours, and driving while intoxicated were increased. New penalties were introduced, and existing ones expanded, for violation of rules governing state trade in alcoholic beverages, producing or buying home-distilled "*samogon,*" and speculating in alcoholic beverages. Parents' responsibility for intoxication of children was increased and managers were made responsible for workers drinking on the job or reporting for work drunk. Fines for various violations were doubled or tripled. Categories of drinkers placed in prison-like "Medical and Labor Rehabilitation" camps were expanded, and the legal proceedings necessary for confinement were simplified.

The government also announced that, starting in 1986, the production of vodka was to be gradually reduced and that the production of fortified fruit wines would be phased out by 1988.

In August 1985, three months after the start of the campaign, prices of alcoholic beverages were, seemingly as an afterthought, raised 15–

Vladimir G. Treml is professor of economics at Duke University.

25 percent.[3] One year later, in August 1986, prices were raised again by 20–25 percent.[4] We will discuss the price policy later and should note here that by August 1986 a liter of average vodka was priced at about 18.50 rubles, a prohibitively high price considering the fact that the average hourly pay in the state sector was about 1.25 rubles.

Compared to these strongly punitive and restrictive measures, the antidrinking campaign offered relatively little in the way of positive policies. One positive element has been the absence of the sort of rhetoric that characterized earlier antidrinking campaigns; the tone of speeches and pronouncements is somber, and the failures of earlier campaigns are admitted. The more pragmatic approach can be seen in the tacit recognition that the boredom of everyday life in the USSR, and the lack of adequate relaxation and entertainment facilities, have been among the factors fostering heavy drinking. To rectify this, the authorities promised to assist in the expansion of athletics and to encourage gardening, home crafts, and hobby activities. Municipalities were directed to establish more sport and athletic facilities, while industry was told to expand the production of home tools, spare parts and components, hobby kits, etc. Transformation of bars and restaurants into nonalcoholic establishments was promised. The authorities also ordered a rapid increase in production of soft drinks and juices and lowered their prices by some 23 percent.[5] It was expected that widely available soft drinks and ice cream would serve as substitutes for alcohol and also absorb some cash that would have been spent on alcoholic beverages.

The antidrinking campaign could not have started too soon. By any comparative, historical, or world health standard, the Soviet Union by the mid–1980s was facing an alcohol problem of truly crisis proportions.

Between 1960 and the mid–1980s consumption more than doubled, reaching a level of 15–16 liters of absolute alcohol per person 15 years of age and older.[6] What makes these high figures particularly alarming is that about two-thirds of this alcohol is consumed in the form of strong alcoholic beverages, i.e., vodka. Several antidrinking campaigns were launched during this period, but they mainly resulted in higher prices for alcoholic beverages and increases in restrictive and punitive measures. Meanwhile, the state alcohol industry continued to expand the production of alcohol and alcoholic beverages and the state retail trade network continued to promote their sale.

Time and space do not allow for a comprehensive discussion of the direct and indirect adverse effects of drinking, so a short summary must suffice.

Soviet and Western demographers agree that heavy drinking has contributed significantly to increasing mortality in the USSR and to such alarming phenomena as the drop in male life expectancy by some four years since the late 1960s.[7]

In the early 1980s direct and indirect deaths from alcohol probably accounted for about one-fifth of all deaths in the country. In some categories alcohol-related mortality in the USSR was well beyond the range of world experience. For example, the number of deaths from acute alcohol poisoning in the late 1970s was a staggering 51,000. This translates to 19.5 deaths per 100,000 of population, compared with a rate of about 0.3 for some 19 countries for which such data are available.[8] In the early 1980s drunken drivers were responsible for 13,000–14,000 traffic deaths and 60,000 serious injuries per year,[9] and some 800,000 drivers were being arrested annually for drunken driving.[10] The rate of arrests per million vehicle-miles was 10 times higher than in the United States.[11] In the late 1970s some 15 million adults were being arrested and placed in sobering-up stations each year.[12]

Heavy drinking and alcohol abuse were major contributing factors in the growth of violent and property crime, divorce, the spread of venereal disease, mental illnesses, suicides, and other social pathologies.

Particularly disturbing to the leadership was the adverse impact of alcohol on labor discipline and labor productivity. The Soviet Union has experienced a continuous decline in the rates of growth of labor productivity since the late 1950s, and it seems reasonable to speculate that one of the major contributing factors was the rapid increase in drinking, particularly drinking on the job. We do not have sufficiently accurate and detailed statistics to isolate and measure the effect of alcohol on the labor force. It should be noted, however, that in the early 1970s two prominent Soviet economists estimated that drinking reduced labor productivity by some 10 percent.[13] We cannot verify these estimates, but, if they were even roughly correct, a similar measure for the mid–1980s could easily have reached 15–17 percent.[14]

It should be added that the existence of a large alcohol underground market has long frustrated government antidrinking policies. A combination of high prices and numerous restrictions on the sale and consumption of alcoholic beverages led to the creation of this large and flourishing market. The main—but by far not the only—element in this market is the illegal home distillation of moonshine, or *samogon*. In the early 1980s production of *samogon* was estimated at over two billion liters per year and accounted for close to 30 percent of total consumption of beverages in all forms converted to pure alcohol.[15] The illegal home producers were also making grape and fruit wines, beer, and a variety of bogus vodkas from stolen technical alcohol. Restrictions on sales fostered speculation, that is, the reselling of alcoholic beverages at a premium by middlemen during hours when the stores were closed or in locations where sales were prohibited. Various abuses in stores and restaurants, such as serving minors and drunks for a premium and shortchanging customers, were also common, as was the widespread theft of alcoholic beverages from the industry and from the distribution network.

The illegal home production of *samogon* and the circumvention of rules governing sales of alcohol by middlemen and dishonest sales personnel in liquor stores and restaurants were seriously limiting the effectiveness of state alcohol policies.

The combination of these factors—high per capita consumption, alarming deterioration of the health of the population caused by heavy drinking, public disorder, stagnating labor productivity, and the large number of moonshiners and speculators openly flouting the law—created what in the eyes of the new General Secretary was an intolerable situation. It is not surprising that Gorbachev assigned such a high priority to antidrinking policies and has been pursuing them so vigorously.

Gorbachev's modernization program and the economic plans for 1986–1990 are keyed to very rapid (in the opinion of many Western observers, unrealistically rapid) increases in labor productivity. Managerial reforms and changes in the labor incentive system or the projected selected increases in capital investment clearly would not be sufficient to provide the planned boost in labor productivity. Thus, expectations of a significant reduction in the adverse effects of alcohol abuse and, particularly, in the premature mortality of men of working age are probably basic to Gorbachev's projections of rapid labor productivity increases.

The new restrictive measures and policies are being enforced with vigor. Central authorities—the Central Committee of the Party, the *Prokuratura*, and the courts—continue to examine the progress of the campaign and issue periodic reports commending regions, agencies, and officials who have succeeded in reducing drinking, while castigating others for laxity. A number of officials have been removed for drinking.[16]

The MVD police apparatus and millions of members of volunteer ''people's squads'' have been mobilized in the all-out attack on alcohol abuse.[17] The police are engaged in sweeping searches and confiscations of home distillation apparatuses, stepped-up arrests for public drunkenness and placement of drunks and heavy drinkers in sobering-up stations, expanded checks of drivers for signs of intoxication, monitoring the enforcement of new regulations in retail trade stores and public eating facilities, keeping order in long and unruly liquor store lines, and apprehending trade personnel and speculators who sell vodka during off hours or in restricted localities.

Fragmentary evidence gleaned from newspapers shows how extensive the police effort is and how widespread are instances of what we would call violations of civil rights. Thus, we read about policemen checking customers' passports before allowing them to enter liquor stores, watching for purchases of excessive numbers of bottles of vodka or large quantities of sugar (the presumption being that sugar is being purchased for home distillation of *samogon*), checking the buyers of aftershave and other alcohol-based lotions, stopping buses and administering breathalizer tests to all adult passengers, or being posted inside restaurants to check passports and observe the guests.[18]

Publicity and propaganda

The immense Soviet propaganda apparatus was fully mobilized for the promotion of sobriety, exposure of the dangers of alcohol, and investigation of local compliance with new rules and regulations. Virtually every newspaper, magazine, and journal began publishing endless articles and stories depicting the horrors of alcohol abuse or dealing with local drunkards.

''*Glasnost'*,'' i.e., the open and frank discussion of existing economic and social problems of the country demanded by Gorbachev, is reflected in the antidrinking campaign only in a limited manner. Press coverage of the campaign is extensive. Much more is being said about drinking and alcohol abuse than in the past, and the tone of the attacks on drinkers is much harsher. The alcohol industry, vineyards, and beer breweries are attacked for producing ''poison.'' The media frequently carry reports about violations of the new regulations by liquor stores and restaurants, enterprise managers (identified by name) who are tolerating drinking by their subordinates on the job, policemen who have been derelict in their duties, and even high-ranking party and state officials dismissed because of drinking. The press has also exposed instances of people who were signed up without their knowledge—by eager managers—with the Voluntary Temperance Society. In this regard we should note what may be the first significant turning point in policies governing the release of potentially embarrassing statistics in the USSR. The 1985 annual statistical compendium, *Narodnoe khoziaistvo*, published detailed data on production and consumption of different alcoholic beverages measured in liters of actual alcohol, and a series on per capita consumption of absolute alcohol.[19]

But all the millions of words published about alcohol notwithstanding, the Soviet population is still as much in the dark as ever about the basic facts and the magnitude of the alcohol problem facing it. Such simple facts as nation-wide statistics on alcohol-related mortality and morbidity, arrests of disorderly drunks, production of illegal home-made alcohol, or on-road accidents caused by drunken drivers are not published in popular or professional literature. Data on ruble sales of alcoholic beverages and on shares of family budgets spent on liquor are also unknown. In fact, a strong case can be made for explaining the public and state complacency concerning the alcohol problem facing the nation by the twenty-year blackout on all meaningful summary information on the production, consumption, and effects of alcohol.

The centrally orchestrated and tightly controlled press campaign of today stresses several key themes and does not allow any discussion of opposing views.

One key theme that emerged in this propaganda blitz concerned the necessity of total abstinence. It must be recalled that for years Soviet specialists have been debating the issue of the acceptable level of drinking. One group consists mainly of medical and legal specialists who conduct research and write on problems of alcohol. This group took a more pragmatic approach, suggesting that most ill effects of alcohol and alcohol abuse in the country would disappear if the drinkers were to learn how to drink in moderation, in a civilized manner (*"kul'-turno"*), i.e., in smaller quantities and spread over longer periods of time, and to combine alcohol with food intake. The opponents took a rather dogmatic position that any amount of alcohol ingested under any conditions was dangerous and detrimental to the individual and the society, and that only total abstinence could save the country.

The Central Committee resolution set the tone for the whole campaign by rejecting the "civilized moderate drinking" idea,[20] and the propaganda apparatus fully embraced the dogmatic position. The notion of civilized drinking was ridiculed in article after article, while its earlier proponents were deprecated and harshly criticized. Once the antidrinking campaign was started, the genuine discussion ceased. The proponents of moderate drinking, such as Boris and Mikhail Levins, E. A. Babaian,[21] and Z. Balaian, who over the years had made major contributions to the literature on alcohol problems, were silenced. The advocates of total abstinence criticize most Soviet specialists, including prominent sociologists and psychiatrists, even for attempted analyses of causes of drinking, implying that explanation may be used as justification of alcohol abuse. The attacks on the position of moderates are in fact becoming more and more a witch-hunt.

A prominent Leningrad surgeon, Fedor Uglov, emerged as the main spokesman for the total abstinence cause. Uglov has long been known as an outspoken critic of all forms of alcohol drinking, but, because of his extreme views, simplistic solutions, and his lack of professional credentials, he was largely ignored by serious Soviet specialists in the past. At the beginning of the campaign Uglov rose to prominence, was appointed as one of the editors of the magazine *Sobriety and Culture* and to the Central Council of the All-Union Voluntary Temperance Society, and proceeded to advocate his views in a style that reminds one of Lysenko.[22] Uglov has many followers in style and substance. One investigative journalist, for example, wrote an "exposé" of two pamphlets on antidrinking education that had been published in the early 1980s by the Ministry of Health of the USSR. The pamphlets contained what from my own point of view are sound suggestions (such as: "Anti-alcohol education should not be reduced to condemnation of alcohol but should help young people to develop a cautious attitude toward it and knowledge of all alcohol characteristics and the existing culture of consumption"). The journalist rudely castigated the authors of the pamphlets, the editor who let these suggestions slip into the text, and the organizations that approved the publication, none of whom had a chance to defend themselves.[23]

The real goals of the antidrinking campaign are not quite clear. Neither the initial May 1985 announcement, nor the subsequent statements made by the Central Committee in its review of the progress of the campaign[24] and by Gorbachev himself are very clear on this point. References to the need to "uproot heavy drinking," "combat alcohol abuse," and make "sobriety the norm of life" seem to suggest that the goal of the campaign is to reduce the consumption of alcohol in the country to an unspecified low level at which all or most negative aspects of drinking would disappear. The main theme of the propaganda campaign, however, is the desirability of total abstinence, and there is other evidence that this, indeed, may be the goal.[25]

Another important theme of the propaganda effort focuses on the Russian or Slavic tradition of drinking. Excessive drinking and alcohol abuse in the USSR are indeed primarily, although not exclusively, a Slavic phenomenon.[26] In the past a number of Soviet and Western scholars drew the unavoidable conclusion that one of the major roots of the high alcohol consumption in the contemporary Soviet Union is the long history of heavy drinking and alcohol abuse in Russia. Among the fruits of this long tradition is the popular notion that drinking is somehow sanctified by Russian history. The reemergence of Russian nationalism in the 1960s probably reinforced this notion. Drinking was recognized, or recognized again, as a time-honored and indispensable element of the Russian way of life. Since the early 1960s the alcohol industry has exploited this popular association of drinking with the Russian past by selecting such brand names for vodka as "Starorusskaia" (Old Russian), "Slavianskaia" (Slavic), "Kazatskaia" (Cossack), "Rossiiskaia" (Russian), and "Zolotoe kol'tso" (The Golden Ring),[27] that is, names invoking positive historical images and appealing to nationalism.

Resurgent Russian chauvinism, accompanied by the desire to present Russia's past in a more favorable light, created a dilemma for propagandists who sought new avenues and approaches in the struggle with alcoholism. To expose the long history of heavy drinking in Russia would be unpopular, no matter what the historical evidence showed. So, the propagandists decided to rewrite history. Articles began to appear explaining that vodka came to Russia rather late and that the majority of Russians had not been heavy drinkers.[28] Appealing to the standard attribute of chauvinism—xenophobia—the propaganda campaign placed blame on foreigners for introducing vodka to Russia and then creating the myth of heavy drinking in Russia. Thus we read:

> "[T]hey were always drinking in Russia. At weddings and at wakes . . . How can one do without? Tradition, custom cannot be overcome." This is exactly the stereotype which foreign propaganda was hammering into our heads. Such talk is a dirty slander on the Russian people, for whom drinking never was a good tradition.[29]

The antidrinking zealots found yet another target. Claiming that drinking was too often presented in a favorable light in the literature and the arts, they began a "clean-up" campaign. By the end of 1987 more than 50 films were completely banned from Soviet theaters on this account; drinking scenes were cut down or out in about 100 television shows.[30]

The magazine *Sobriety and Culture* of the newly created All-Union Voluntary Temperance Society appears to be addressing mainly the Slavic readership. It offers a mix of articles on Russian folklore, stresses positive elements of Russian history, and appeals to national pride. Russian traditional themes, antidrinking folk sayings and proverbs, and pictures of typically Slavic beauties in ethnic costumes are interspersed with promotion of healthy pursuits such as sports and outdoor folk games, recipes for Slavic folk dishes, healthy substitutes for alcohol such as tea and fruit drinks, and suggestions for restoration of pagan (and nondrinking) rites and dances.

So far, the first twelve issues of the magazine have not dealt with any foreign topics, with one rather revealing and ominous exception. The third issue published an article titled "The Logic of Violence and Degradation,"[31] which described Israel as a country torn by racism, crime, corruption, drugs, and alcohol abuse, and featured a composite color picture showing three bottles, guns, and a pile of white powder (cocaine?). Attacks on Israel are not new in the Soviet media, but why publish one in this magazine, which had not previously dealt with foreign issues? Why select Israel, which has one of the lowest per capita alcohol consumption levels in the world? It is possible that the inclusion of this article was accidental. But one can also speculate that the new anti-alcohol magazine with its emphasis on things Russian was attempting to exploit the latent anti-Semitism of its readers. In the past one element among the complex roots of anti-Semitism was the contempt of hard-drinking Russians for the non-drinking Jew. Now that the editors of *Sobriety and Culture* have declared that true Russians do not and never did drink, and that abstinence is commendable, would it not make sense for them to find that Israelis, i.e., Jews, do drink? This bothersome question must remain open, but somehow the appearance of this anti-Israel article does not seem accidental.[32]

This exploitation of anti-Semitism, the rather crude rewriting of Russian history to create an image of a sober country, the scare tactics of the propaganda, and the promotion of the total abstinence goal to the exclusion of all other views suggest that the principles of Gorbachev's "*glasnost'*" are not applied uniformly.

Fiscal constraints

One problem faced by Soviet authorities in the course of pursuing the goals of the antidrinking campaign is fiscal. In the USSR, as in tsarist Russia, the state monopoly on alcohol has provided a major share of state budgetary revenues. Taxes on alcoholic beverages, earnings from profitable foreign trade in alcohol, and taxes on profits of the alcohol industry were conservatively estimated by the author in 1982 at 42 billion rubles, or some 12 percent of all state revenues; this share remained at about the same level or was even somewhat higher on the eve of the campaign.[33] Since one ruble of sales of alcoholic beverages generates about 0.83 rubles of revenues, any appreciable cut in sales would result in a proportional drop in budgetary revenues.[34] Exact calculations are difficult, but for illustrative purposes we could say that a 40-percent reduction in sales of alcoholic beverages would result in losses to the budget that approximately equal the annual budgetary expenditure for public health and physical education.

But the destabilizing results of such cuts go beyond direct losses to the budget. Since in the short run the state cannot replace losses in alcohol sales by increased production and sale of consumer goods, and since it appears that no serious price or tax reform is contemplated by the authorities in the near future, we have to conclude that most rubles not spent on alcohol will remain unspent. Increased liquidity in the hands of the consumers would then add to the suppressed inflation, reduce incentives to work, and have other undesirable effects.

While the Soviet authorities must have been aware of this potential problem of revenue loss, there is no evidence that any measures to counteract it had been considered at the start of the campaign, except for vague hopes that the increased production of soft drinks and juices and sales of consumer goods from "inner reserves" would cushion the shock. This clearly did not happen.

The restriction, higher penalties, and closing of a number of liquor stores and restaurants announced in May 1985 had immediate effects. Several cities reported that sales of alcoholic beverages were off 25 to 30 percent,[35] indicating that the campaign had at least a successful start. Unexpectedly, the authorities announced in August that prices of alcoholic beverages were to be increased by 25–30 percent;[36] this must have been necessitated by the revenue loss.[37]

Virtually the same puzzling action was taken about a year later. Speaking at the end of July, Gorbachev reported that in the first six months of 1986 the sales of alcoholic beverages fell off by an additional 35 percent. He noted that this drop in sales resulted in a budgetary loss of 5 billion rubles, but expressed his confidence that this loss would somehow be covered.[38] Five days later the Chairman of the State Committee on Prices, Glushkov, announced that prices of alcoholic beverages were being raised by 20–25 percent.[39]

We do not know, of course, what happens behind the closed doors of the Ministry of Finance, or at the Politburo meetings, but both price increases are puzzling. They were clearly not needed to discourage sales, because sales were dropping anyway; they can be explained only by considerations of fiscal expediency. Higher prices for alcoholic beverages at this stage of the antidrinking campaign will probably prove to be counterproductive, inasmuch as they provide an additional profit incentive to illegal home producers of *samogon*.

The fact that the influential Chairman of the State Committee on Prices was retired without honors three weeks after announcing the price increase[40] only adds to the mystery and reinforces one's speculation that the whole campaign was hastily prepared and policies of different government agencies had not been coordinated.

Results

The immediate results of the antidrinking campaign were, at least from the point of view of the authorities, encouraging.

Higher prices, restrictions, stiffer penalties, closing down of about half the liquor stores, and prohibition of serving alcohol in a large number of restaurants led to a significant reduction in sales. According to official Soviet statistics, in the June–December 1985 period sales were down by 25 percent compared with the same period in 1984,[41] and in the first six months of 1986 sales were further reduced by 37 percent.[42] Consumption of absolute alcohol on a per capita basis in 1985 was reduced by about 15 percent compared with 1984.[43] Tentative estimates made by the author indicate that per capita consumption of state-produced alcoholic beverages in 1986 was about 5.6 liters of absolute alcohol—a remarkable 50 percent reduction compared with 1984. Surveys conducted by the Ministry of Trade indicated that as a result of the campaign 12 percent of drinkers completely stopped drinking, 36 percent reduced the level of alcohol consumed, and 52 percent continued to drink without a change.[44]

It is difficult to assess accurately the results of this reduction in drinking, since most general statements made by authorities are somewhat vague and, in some instances at least, subject to alternative interpretations.

Various Soviet sources suggest that, generally speaking, there has been a significant decline in the adverse effects of alcohol abuse.

Gorbachev himself reported with obvious satisfaction that the number of accidental deaths caused by drinking was reduced by 20 percent and the number of divorces resulting from drinking by one of the spouses was also down.[45]

The Deputy Chairman of the Supreme Court of the USSR, S. Gusev, reported that the percentage of convicted criminals who were intoxicated at the time of the crime declined from 53 percent in the 1980–1984 period to 49 percent in 1985.[46]

There are some conflicting reports on the total number of traffic accidents, but it appears that the share of accidents caused by drunken drivers dropped from 28.6 percent of all accidents in 1984 to 24.6 percent in 1985.[47] However, such statistics could be misleading. For example, there have been reports that some drivers, afraid of being charged with drunken driving, are engaged in a somewhat bizarre practice of using enemas to ingest vodka rectally. Apparently, this method provides for the desired intoxication effect without being detectable by police breathalyzer tests.[48] It is difficult to say how often this takes place, but it does illustrate the possibility of distortions in statistics of social anomalies; that is, instances of drunken driving and accidents caused by intoxicated drivers could decline statistically but not necessarily in real life.

A large number of newspaper reports suggests that open street drinking and alcohol abuse are declining: there are fewer drunkards in the streets and fewer are placed in sobering-up stations, the number of disturbances of public peace by drunkards is down, and drinking on the job has declined. The number of official banquets and receptions at which alcohol is served was drastically down, and generally more entertainment was taking place without alcohol, as in the growing number of "alcohol-free weddings."

The economy performed better in 1986, and labor productivity increased,[49] but we do not have enough information to evaluate these improvements fully. It would in any case be premature to expect statistically significant improvement that could be attributed to the anti-drinking campaign, and none of the Soviet leaders have made such claims.

What can be said about these short-term results?

In the first place we should note that some of these results may be, and in all probability are, exaggerated, or at least presented in a somewhat distorted manner.

Let us examine, for example, the drop in divorces proudly reported by Gorbachev. We do not know the magnitude of this decline, but most specialists would probably agree that even a significant cut in alcohol consumption, no matter how distributed, is not likely to produce a statistically significant drop in the divorce rate within one year. Thus the reported decline in the divorce rate associated with the antidrinking campaign looks doubtful. But we have direct evidence explaining this phenomenon. According to a report from the Ul'ianovsk region, the authorities established special "reconciliation commissions" which investigated all divorce applications and succeeded in convincing 1,000 out of 5,000 couples to withdraw their applications.[50] It does not really matter what kind of pressures these commissions (organized mainly at places of employment) applied. The simple fact is that this reduction in divorces is explained by an administrative intervention and not by the reduction in levels of alcohol abuse. It should be added, moreover, that the total number of divorces actually increased by 10,000 in 1986.[51] It is thus possible that the decline reported by Gorbachev was caused by the fact that, under pressures produced by the campaign, fewer couples seeking divorce listed drinking as the reason.

Similarly, doubts are raised about the importance of the increase in the number of "alcohol-free weddings" when we read an account of promises made, by the director of a factory employing an engaged couple, to provide the newlyweds with a new apartment (to which they were not entitled otherwise) if they would agree not to serve alcohol at their wedding.[52]

There is also some evidence of outright falsification of the reported results of the antidrinking campaign.[53]

An assessment of the results of Gorbachev's antidrinking campaign should be based not on isolated phenomena but rather on the overall picture, and here is where we do not yet have sufficiently accurate and comprehensive data. However, the emerging evidence suggests that, at least in the short run, the campaign has not produced any lasting positive results.

It must be emphasized that heavy drinking and alcohol abuse, particularly of the magnitude observed in the USSR and in light of its deep historical roots there, is a multidimensional and a highly complex phenomenon which cannot be eliminated or even significantly moderated in a span of one or two years by a set of relatively crude punitive measures and restrictions. World experience shows that modification of behavior achieved by such measures results, more often than not, in the emergence of unanticipated negative effects in other spheres of social life.

To illustrate this point, let us examine some of the unexpected effects of the antidrinking campaign. Consumption of state-made alcoholic beverages was drastically reduced by cuts in production, higher prices, and restrictions on distribution and sales. However, despite increased penalties and intensified police efforts, production of *samogon* and homemade wine and beer has been rapidly increasing. The manufacturing process of home distillation is very simple, prices of ingredients are low,[54] and the 70-percent increase in the price of vodka allowed the home distillers to boost the price of *samogon* sufficiently to compensate for the increased risk factor. According to B. Zabotin, Deputy Minister of Internal Affairs (MVD), sales of *samogon* increased by some 42 percent and home production of wine tripled in the first ten months of 1986.[55] Using these figures, the author has tentatively estimated that in 1986 consumption of *samogon* on a per capita basis grew by some 40 percent. This means that the actual per capita consumption of alcohol in all forms (i.e., state-produced and home-made) has declined during the campaign by only 23–25 percent and not 50 percent as reported by official sources. This remarkably rapid growth of illegal distillation seems incredible, but we find confirmation in the Soviet media. Thus, it was reported that in Kazakhstan, seven out of ten drunks placed in sobering-up stations had been drinking *samogon* and that generally "reduction in consumption of state-produced alcoholic beverages was more than covered by increases in consumption of home-made liquor."[56] Describing the increased police efforts in the struggle with illegal producers, the Minister of Internal Affairs, A. Vlasov, sounded both alarmed and pessimistic about the prospects for the future.[57] Increased consumption of *samogon* means that sugar and other products are being diverted from food consumption, and that drinking will have even greater adverse effects on health, because home-produced beverages contain more impurities.

Of course, the higher prices of state-produced and home-distilled beverages do discourage some drinkers. Unfortunately, the most desperate ones are forced to switch to drinking alcohol surrogates, the least harmful of which are aftershave lotions and colognes.[58] Runs on lotions and alcohol-based medicines have become so frequent that some stores restrict sales to two bottles per customer, some restrict the hours of sale, and some have had to call in police to control unruly buyers.[59] Much more harmful are technical alcohol, antifreeze, methanol, and other toxic fluids, which are consumed in increasing quantities. Not surprisingly, the number of reported fatal alcohol poisonings is also increasing.[60] Thus, we read of five deaths from methanol in one factory,[61] and about a case of 32 people who were poisoned—15 of them died—from drinking stolen antifreeze.[62]

The sharp increases in prices of all alcoholic beverages pushed up the premiums paid on state-produced beverages in black-market distribution, thus compensating middlemen and retail trade personnel for additional risk. In an earlier study the author estimated that before the start of the campaign, the premium on vodka sold after hours by retail trade personnel and by taxi drivers (to people who did not want to wait in long lines) was 50 percent. Recent reports indicate that black-market vodka now sells at about twice the store price.[63] Various new methods of circumventing the restrictions have appeared. As a "service" to people who want to avoid hours of queuing, speculators take a place in a line and sell it for several rubles just before entering the store. In some allegedly non–alcohol-serving restaurants, vodka is sold under the guise of mineral water if one pays the waiter the price difference.[64]

Another important issue that seems to alarm the authorities is the increasing use of narcotics and the possibility that many alcohol users deterred by higher prices, restrictions, penalties, and public opprobrium are switching from alcohol to drugs. Very little is known about drug abuse in the USSR, but, to judge by the rapid increase in the media coverage of the problem, the use of drugs is growing.[65] The relationships between narcotics and alcohol are highly complex, and the experience in the West does not indicate the existence of a strong substitutability between the two substances. Nonetheless, Soviet specialists seem to be convinced that narcotics are being used as a substitute for alcohol. The Deputy Minister of Health of the RSFSR reported unequivocally that users switch from one to another depending on supply[66]; while the Deputy Chairman of the State Committee on Prices said that he believed that higher alcohol prices and cuts in production have led to an increase in the use of narcotics.[67]

More numerous police patrols and sharply increased penalties have brought a significant reduction in the numbers of drunks seen in the streets and of disturbances of public peace, which, needless to say, must be a welcome relief for the average person in the streets. However, it is difficult to say whether the society has benefited. Thus, newspapers report that drinkers now stay at home or in their dormitories, causing more problems in the family environment, more cases of wife and child abuse and of property destruction, and at the same time, making police intervention more difficult.[68]

The same phenomenon of substitution of one adverse effect of heavy drinking by another is observed in many other areas.

Thus, while drinking on the job has been cut down, labor mobility has increased as workers fired from one enterprise for drinking get hired by another.[69]

Another example is found in the medical field. According to regulations dating back to the late 1970s but strengthened in 1985, people who suffer injuries while intoxicated or as the result of intoxication are denied sick leave by their enterprises and in certain cases have to pay for their treatment. To avoid these penalties, people now delay reporting for medical treatment of injuries sustained while drunk until they have sobered up.[70] Thus, while statistically the number of accidents associated with alcohol is down, the true health impact of such accidents is more severe, as delayed treatment creates medical complications.

The rapid reduction in the production of alcoholic beverages and in the number of distribution outlets has not been without cost.

The grape-growing and vodka- and wine-producing industries are in a shambles. Some 90 percent of Soviet vineyards grow wine grapes, and the projected shift to table variety grapes entails destruction of existing vines and replanting of millions of acres. The closing down of a large number of vodka and wine plants and of liquor stores resulted in temporary unemployment and the need to retrain and to relocate workers. Wine-producing regions and republics (the North Caucasus, the Ukraine, Moldavia, Georgia, and Azerbaijan) were affected particularly strongly. The Georgian wine industry's output was cut by 50 percent,[71] which means a serious loss of income for the republic. Conversion of now closed vodka and wine factories to production of soft drinks and juices is costly and simply cannot be effected in all cases.

Expansion of the production of fruit juices and soft drinks will, needless to say, be welcomed by the consumer. However, the expectations that soft drinks will replace alcoholic beverages and ease the pain of withdrawal have no ground.

None of these problems are insurmountable, but they all add to the rising real costs of the antidrinking campaign.

What are the the prospects for the future? There is no doubt that in general a sustained and a well-designed antidrinking campaign encompassing reduced production of alcohol, restrictions on distribution, strict rules controlling drinking, and continuous educational and propaganda efforts will have beneficial results in the long run.

There are, however, several reasons to question the effectiveness of Gorbachev's campaign and the ability of the authorities to maintain its momentum.

The Soviet leadership will have to either increase production of consumer goods and services to absorb the rubles not spent on alcoholic beverages, or launch a major tax, wage, and price reform. Such reforms are difficult to design and to implement and they are not likely to be considered in the immediate future. The authorities' recognition that the boredom of everyday life in the Soviet Union is one of the major reasons for drinking was an important first step. But increased production of hobby kits and spare parts for cars (as called for in the documents announcing the campaign) is far from being a complete answer to this problem. Adequate housing space would appear to be more important for facilitating the expansion of leisure activities. Development of a comprehensive program of expansion of the whole infrastructure of entertainment, relaxation, and rest facilities for the population will be costly and will take the state many years.

The campaign itself has several serious faults that will make themselves felt in the future. World experience suggests that punitive and restrictive measures alone are not effective in combating excessive drinking; they must be combined with positive policies and expansion of treatment, psychiatric and social counseling, and rehabilitation services. The long tradition of refusing to consider alcoholism a disease—still widely shared by state authorities and public health officials in the USSR—resulted in poorly funded and staffed facilities for treatment of alcoholics and people with developing alcohol dependence. The newly created narcological service network is inadequate and has little prospect of improvement in the immediate future. In short, the focus and the emphasis of the antidrinking campaign is on punitive and restrictive measures, and public health issues have been barely mentioned.

The effects of the intensive propaganda campaign, which is designed to depict the evils of drinking and to frighten the public with pictures of moral and physical degradation resulting from alcohol, are difficult to assess at this time. The experience of many countries suggests that scare tactics of this nature are not an effective method of dealing with such complex phenomena as alcohol abuse. Several surveys conducted among younger people in Novosibirsk before the start of the campaign and at the end of 1985 produced mixed results. In some instances, the surveys showed that the campaign has actually increased the tendency to drink.[72]

The goal of total abstinence is completely unrealistic, given the long history of alcohol culture in the USSR. The removal from positions of authority and the silencing of prominent Soviet specialists who counseled gradual approaches to the alcohol problem and put the stress on teaching moderation to drinkers was a serious mistake.[73]

The two major increases in prices of alcoholic beverages (which, I believe, had not been included in the original design of the campaign and were forced on the authorities by fiscal considerations) were not necessary and were, in fact, counterproductive. Soviet experience of the late 1950s showed that major price increases did not discourage drinking but simply forced heavy drinkers and people with alcohol dependence to curtail their expenditures of other consumer goods and services, often at the expense of the welfare of their families. Price increases also encouraged the expansion of illegal home distillation, theft of alcohol, and other activities of the alcohol underground whose existence frustrates the authorities and places additional burdens on the police.

The whole campaign was clearly prepared hastily and with naive expectations of rapid results—particularly, improvements in work discipline and labor productivity. In this respect the authorities will be disappointed, as in all probability the real economic and social costs of the campaign will continue to rise and the potential benefits will not begin to be felt for several years. So far, even in the face of growing costs and obvious dissatisfaction on the part of at least some segments of the population, the campaign has not slowed down.[74] The test of Gorbachev's power and control over the bureaucracy will lie in his ability to maintain the momentum of this campaign, the benefits of which are still uncertain.

Notes

1. This study is based on sources that were available through early 1987. The antidrinking campaign is far from over yet, and thus this study and its conclusions must be considered as preliminary. The author is grateful to professors

Murray Feshbach, Maurice Friedberg, Gregory Grossman, Aron Katsenelinboigen, and David Powell for comments and suggestions made at different stages of drafting of this paper. The responsibility for errors of fact and interpretation is, of course, the author's.

2. See *Pravda*, 17 May 1985, 1, for the resolution of the Central Committee, announcement of the Council of Ministers, and the decree by the Supreme Soviet. A summary of these and subsequent laws and regulations dealing with alcohol is found in Stolbov, ed., 1985.

3. Radio Moscow, 26 August 1985.

4. *Pravda*, 1 August 1986, 3.

5. *Izvestiia*, 15 August 1985, 5.

6. See *Narodnoe khoziaistvo* 1986, 609, and Treml 1987, A4–A17. As will be discussed below, statistics on alcohol consumption had been long suppressed in the USSR, and the author had to estimate them from a variety of sources. After the author's 1986 study was completed, per capita data appeared in the USSR, and they were very close to author's earlier estimates. The figure of 15–16 liters of absolute alcohol given above includes consumption of state-produced alcoholic beverages as well as estimated consumption of homemade alcohol.

7. See Feshbach 1982, 34. Feshbach's estimates were recently broadly confirmed by newly released Soviet data in *Narodnoe khoziaistvo* 1985, 547.

8. Treml 1987, 44–45.

9. Gusev 1986, 57.

10. *Pravda*, 12 July 1983, 3.

11. Treml 1987, 46.

12. Treml 1987, 62.

13. Strumilin and Sonin 1974, 38.

14. One Soviet author estimated losses in the 1980s at 15–20 percent (Zagoruiko 1987, 117).

15. See Treml 1985 for a description and analysis of the alcohol underground. Estimates on consumption of *samogon* are by necessity rather rough. However, a recent Soviet article reported that in the mid-1980s "illegal home distillation uses up more than one million tons of sugar annually" (Bazhenov 1985, 11). This figure is fully consistent with the author's estimates.

16. The numbers of those arrested or otherwise penalized are large. For example, 455 party officials were reprimanded and 74 were expelled from the Party in Vinnitsa Oblast (*Pravda*, 24 September 1985, 3); in Estonia in a span of two months 700 people (half of whom were administrators) were arrested for drinking on the job (*Sotsialisticheskaia zakonnost'* 1986 [10], 34); and in Moscow, the *Prokuratura* inspected 47 technical schools and penalized 330 teachers for drunkenness (*Uchitel'skaia gazeta*, 25 September 1986, 2).

17. The total number of these auxiliary policemen, or *druzhinniki*, was reported at fourteen million (Vlasov 1987, 10). Some of these squads are probably inactive or exist only on paper, and Western observers and the Soviet media report that "people's squads" are quite visible in apprehending drunks, stopping drunken fights, and checking drinking establishments.

18. *Literaturnaia gazeta*, 7 May 1986, 11; *Izvestiia*, 11 April 1986, 3; *Pravda*, 27 April 1986, 6.

19. *Narodnoe khoziaistvo* 1986, 254, 471, and 609.

20. *Pravda*, 17 May 1985, 1.

21. Babaian's case is particularly distressing. The author of several important books and a long list of articles on alcoholism, Babaian started to sound the alarm concerning the dangers of drinking at the time when most public health officials were silent. Refusing to recognize his expertise in the field of alcoholism, the authorities kept him in the position of the head of a section on foreign medical technologies in the Ministry of Health of the USSR. His recognition came in the late 1970s when he was appointed to direct the newly created network of narcological services. In October 1985 Babaian was selected as the scapegoat for the lack of effectiveness of the public health establishment in the struggle with alcoholism. The Control Committee of the Central Committee of the CPSU reviewing the work of the Ministry singled him out with a severe reprimand (*Pravda*, 30 October 1985, 3). His name has since disappeared from print.

22. For a sample of Uglov's writing see *Izvestiia* 4 June 1984, 3, and Uglov 1986. Uglov's tactics consist in trying to frighten the reader with endless descriptions of horrors of drinking and devastating physiological effects of alcohol without regard to facts or analysis. His attacks are directed not only at most Soviet medical specialists in alcoholism, but even at such trivia as the fact that alcoholic beverages are listed under the food category in the official retail trade classification.

23. Pankrat'eva 1986, 28–30.

24. *Pravda*, 19 September 1985, q1.

25. Thus, the Deputy Minister of Trade of the USSR said in a television interview in April of 1986 that "central authorities plan a reduction in vodka consumption of 300 million liters per year reaching an almost zero production level this century" (JPRS-UPS–86–028, Social Issues, 24 June 1986). The Minister of Health of the Ukrainian republic said in May of the same year that the goal of the campaign is to "outlaw the consumption of vodka by the year 2000" (*RFE/RL Research Bulletin*, 180/86, 2 May 1986).

26. According to *samizdat* sources Gorbachev discussed the antidrinking campaign at a closed meeting with prominent writers. He was quoted as saying: "We must save the people, particularly the Slavic people. This (drinking) has moved to Muslims and to the Caucasus, but no one suffers as much as Slavs, that is, Russians, Ukrainians, and Belorussians" (*Novoe Russkoe Slovo*, 16 November 1986, 4).

27. The Golden Ring refers to the roughly circular position of several historically famous Russian cities such as Moscow, Vladimir, and Suzdal'. Of 26 popular vodkas produced since the early 1960s, 16 have names appealing to nationalistic sentiments.

28. See *Kommunist* 1985, 52–53; Lirmian 1985, 120; Bykov 1985, 107; Seredich 1985, 4. Particularly representative of this type of writing is an article describing an interview with a Soviet historian, V. Buganov, under the title, "The Lie about Drunken Russia: A Soviet Historian Debates Foreign Sovietologists" (Seregin 1985, 2–3).

29. Zaichenko 1985, 2.

30. Chernykh 1987, 3.

31. Demin 1986, 52–54.

32. The evidence is not overwhelming, but there are other signs that at least some officials responsible for the antidrinking propaganda efforts are exploiting anti-Semitism. A book on Zionism published in 1986 in Leningrad resurrected old accusations of Jewish merchants for monopolizing the liquor trade in Russia and inducing Russians to drink (Romanenko 1986). The author was told of, but has not seen, another pamphlet, published in 1986 in the Ukraine, that repeats this.

33. Treml 1987, q112.

34. We are referring to direct losses to the state budget, i.e., cuts in collections of excise taxes on alcoholic beverages and in taxes on profits in the alcohol industry and retail trade. The antidrinking campaign produced other, and probably not insignificant, losses to the whole economy resulting from losses of revenues in retail trade and public dining, from the closing of a large number of vodka- and wine-producing plants or their conversion to production of nonalcoholic beverages, and destruction of vineyards. Some of these losses are affecting wine-producing republics particularly strongly.

35. Zaigraev 1985, 47–48; *Literaturnaia gazeta*, October 2, 1985, 11.

36. Radio Moscow, 26 August 1985.

37. According to reports in the French press (*Le Monde*, 2 February 1986, 5), the chairman of Gosbank complained to the visiting French Minister of Finance of a projected annual loss of state revenues of 12 billion rubles.

38. *Pravda*, 27 July 1986, 2.

39. *Pravda*, 1 August 1986, 3.

40. *Izvestiia*, 19 August 1986, 2.

41. *Trud*, 1 January 1986, 3.

42. *Ekonomicheskaia gazeta*, No. 31, July 1986, 12.

43. *Narodnoe khoziaistvo* 1986, 609.

44. Kogai and Kokorina 1986, 13. We cannot say how large and how well designed the surveys were. The article actually reported that 11 percent stopped, 34 percent cut down, and 49 percent continued to drink as before. The sum of the three values is only 94 percent, which could mean that 6 percent of drinkers increased the amount of alcohol consumed, or that 6 percent of those surveyed did not answer the questions. To be on the conservative side we assumed that the latter was true and therefore recalculated these percentages so that they added up to 100.

45. *Pravda*, 27 July 1986, 2.

46. Gusev 1986, 58. Gusev's statistics are interesting in another respect. Discussing the 53 to 49 percent decline mentioned above, he notes that the absolute number of convicted criminals who were drunk had increased by 20 percent. If his statistics are correct, a simple calculation shows that the total number of convictions in 1985 increased by 30 percent compared with the average number in 1980–1984. This would be an important admission by a ranking Soviet jurist, considering the fact that Soviet sources usually claim a continuous decline in crime.

47. FBIS, *Foreign Press Note*, 30 April 1986.

48. The evidence is based on two references found in the literature (Maksimov 1981, 138, and Morozov *et al.* 1983, 21) and interviews with three recent émigrés.

49. In the first six months of 1986, labor productivity in industry increased by 5.2 percent and in construction by 4.9 percent (*Ekonomicheskaia gazeta*, No. 31, July 1986, 11) compared with, respectively, 3.6 and 2.8 percent average increases in the 1981–1984 period. However, it should be noted that the national statistics showing economic improvements in 1985 and 1986 contain a number of inconsistencies and puzzles, and it is quite possible that performance indicators are being manipulated by authorities to present the results of Gorbachev's leadership in a more favorable light. See Vanous 1986, 1–20, and Hanson 1986, 1–4.

50. Samsonov 1986, 2.

51. *Vestnik statistiki*, No. 1, 1987, 68.

52. Kishkin 1986, 2. The end of the story is disappointing. The couple and the parents were reluctant to agree, particularly since the necessary ten cases of vodka had already been purchased, but they finally capitulated. The wedding without alcohol was a success, but unfortunately the ensuing publicity forced the employer to cancel the apartment deal. The newspaper did not say what happened to the ten cases of vodka.

53. Grineva 1986, 2; *Vozdushnyi transport*, 1986, 4.

54. The increase to 30 kopecks per 100 g. of yeast (*Izvestiia*, 15 August 1985, 2), designed to discourage home distillation, means a 2–3 kopeck increase in the cost of one liter of *samogon*; the black market price went up by some 5 rubles per liter since the beginning of the campaign.

55. Zabotin 1986.

56. Kviatkovskii 1987, 4.

57. Vlasov 1987, 3.

58. According to a police report, drinkers in one district of Rostov Oblast had consumed more than one thousand liters of aftershave lotion and 6,600 liters of *samogon* in the few months since the start of the campaign (*Izvestiia*, 31 January 1986, 3).

59. Rubinov 1986, 12.

60. *Trud*, 13 July 1985, 2; *Sotsialisticheskaia zakonnost'* 1986 (10), 33–36; *Kommunist* (Armeniia), 25 July 1986, 3; Negoda 1986, 2; *Ogonek*, May 1986, 26; Illesh and Makarov 1985, 3; *Izvestiia*, 1 January 1976, 6; *Sotsialisticheskaia industriia*, 30 May 1985, 3, and 9 February 1985, 3; *Trezvost' i kul'tura*, 1986 (3): 51; *Nedelia*, 1986 (30): 4; *Trud*, 15 August 1986, 2; *Izvestiia*, 27 August 1985, 2, and 26 November 1985, 3.

61. *Izvestiia*, 12 September 1985, 4.

62. *Literaturnaia gazeta*, 17 September 1986, 11.

63. Treml 1985, 24. For evidence of speculation in state-produced vodka see *The Observer*, 22 June 1986, 3; *Nedelia*, 1985 (44): 7; *Sotsialisticheskaia zakonnost'*, 1985(11): 32; *Izvestiia*, 10 January 1986, 3; *Izvestiia*, 31 January 1986, 3; *Sotsialisticheskaia industriia*, 2 June 1986, 4; *Trud*, 21 January 1986, 4; *Trud*, 5 September 1986, 2; *Trezvost' i kul'tura*, 1986 (6): 23; *Nedelia*, 1986 (36): 1986, 6.

64. *Ogonek*, 1986 (20): 27.

65. For a sample of reports see *Washington Times*, 22 July 1986, 9; *Ogonek*, 1986 (25): 27–28; *Literaturnaia gazeta*, 20 August 1986, 11; *Izvestiia*, 11 August 1986, 3, and 3 August 1986, 3; *Sovetskaia Rossiia*, 24 August 1986, 3; *Sovetskaia kul'tura*, 20 May 1986, 3; *Moskovskaia Pravda*, 10 April 1986, 2.

66. Potapov 1986, 11.

67. Komin 1986, 3.

68. *Trud*, 19 March 1986, 2; 10 June 1986, 2; 25 July 1986, 2; *Partiinaia zhizn'*, 1985 (21): 68–71; *Pravda*, 7 July 1986, 7; *Izvestiia*, 29 May 1986, 6; *Nedelia*, 1985 (16): 5; 1986 (4): 12; 1986 (36): 6.

69. Starostenko 1985, 2.

70. *Trud*, 11 May 1986, 2.

71. *Pravda*, 22 October l985, 5.

72. Makarov 1987, 128–129.

73. Reaction to the simplistic position of the proponents of total abstinence may be starting. A first modest attempt to justify moderate drinking was made in a popular magazine in 1987 (Ol'shanskii and Batygin 1987, 2–3).

74. Soviet and Western observers have been periodically reporting that the campaign is losing its momentum (Editorial, *Izvestiia*, 10 January 1986, 3; L. Osheverova, *Izvestiia*, 30 June 1986, 6; N. Vorob'ev, *Pravda*, 20 March 1986, 2; Gary Lee, *Washington Post*, 8 December 1986, A16). In December 1986, the strict rules governing liquor trade in Moscow were somewhat relaxed and some closed liquor stores were reopened (*Radio Liberty Research Bulletin*, 85/87, 27 February 1987, 14). So far, this author sees no evidence that the authorities have decided to reverse the antidrinking measures, and the reported instances appear to be insignificant readjustments. In the first three months of 1987 the sales of alcoholic beverages were down some 30 percent compared with the same period in 1986, indicating that the pressures continue. See *Ekonomicheskaia gazeta*, 1987 (18) (April): 10.

Bibliography

The bibliography lists monographs and papers and articles in the periodic literature that present information of broad general interest. Short media reports of single instances or cases are cited in the notes but not listed in the bibliography.

Bazhenov, G. 1985. *Literaturnaia gazeta*, 29 May, 11.
Bykov, A. 1985. *Ekonomika i organizatsiia promyshlennogo proizvodstva* (9): 93–128.
Cheban, I. 1986. *Pravda*, 9 September, 3.
Chernykh, N. S. 1987. *Trezvost' i kul'tura* (1): 2–3.
Demin, V. 1986. *Trezvost' i kul'tura* (3): 52–54.
Feshbach, M. 1982. "The Soviet Union: Population Trends and Dilemmas." *Population Bulletin* 37 (3) (August).
Grineva, N. 1986. *Trud*, 14 August 1986, 2.
Gusev, S. I. 1986. *Sovetskoe gosudarstvo i pravo* (4): 55–63.
Hanson, Ph. 1986. "Puzzles in the 1985 Statistics." *Radio Liberty Research Bulletin*, 439/86 (20 November), 1–4.
Illesh, A., and Makarov, Iu. 1985. *Izvestiia*, 9 December, 3.
Kishkin, N. 1986. *Trud*, 25 March, 2.
Komin, A. N. *Komsomol'skaia Pravda*, 13 August 1986, 3.
Kommunist 1985 (12): 43–54.
Korgai, R., and Kokorin, T. 1986. *Sovetskaia torgovlia* (8): 13–14.
Kviatkovskii, O., 1987. *Trud*, 21 April, 4.
Lirmian, R. 1985. *Kommunist* (8): 113–120.
Makarov, V. 1987. *Ekonomika i organizatsiia promyshlennogo proizvodstva* (1): 118–143.
Maksimov, V. 1981. *Kontinent* (30): 76–172.
Morozov, V. *et al.* 1983. *Alkogolizm: rukovodstvo dlia vrachei*. Moscow.
Narodnoe khoziaistvo SSSR v 1985 godu. Moscow, 1986.
Negoda, G. 1986. *Trud*, 25 July, 2.
Novosadchenko, E. 1986. *Pravda*, 15 June, 3.
Ol'shanskii, V., and G. Batygin. 1987. *Nedelia* (19): 2–3.
Potapov, A. I. 1986. *Literaturnaia gazeta*, 20 August, 11.
Povetkin, O. 1985. *Nedelia* (50): 7.
Romanenko, A. Z. 1986. *Klassovaia sushchnost' sionizma*. Leningrad.
Rubinov, A. 1986. *Literaturnaia gazeta*, 12 November, 12.
Samsonov, Iu. 1986. *Trud*, 20 February, 2.
Seredich, I. 1985. *Sovetskaia Belorussiia*, 12 May, 4.
Seregin, A. 1985. *Sovetskaia Rossiia*, 14 July, 2–3.
Starostenko, V. 1985. *Trud*, 4 December, 2.
Stolbov, B. A., ed. 1985. *Zakonodatel'stvo o bor'be s p'ianstvom i alkogolizmom*, Moscow.
Strumilin, S., and M. Sonin. 1974. *Ekonomika i organizatsiia promyshlennogo proizvodstva* (4): 36–44.
Treml, V. 1985. "Alcohol in the Soviet Underground Economy," *Berkeley-Duke Occasional Papers on the Second Economy in the USSR* (7) (December). Durham, NC.

————. 1987. *Alcohol Abuse and Quality of Life in the USSR* (Study prepared for Georgetown University Project on Quality of Life in the USSR), manuscript, forthcoming.

Uglov, F. G. 1986. *Nash sovremennik* (4): 154–161.

Vanous, J. 1986. "Soviet Economic Performance during the First Half of 1986." *PlanEcon Report* 2 (32–33) (14 August), 1–20.

Vlasov, A. V. 1987. *Izvestiia*, 11 March, 2.

————. 1987. *Literaturnaia gazeta*, 18 March, 10.

Vozdushnyi transport, 8 April 1986, p. 4.

Zabotin, B. 1986. Central TV Program, Moscow, 2 December; reported by *Xinhua* (Beijing), 3 December 1986.

Zagoruiko, N. 1987. *Ekonomika i organizatsiia promyshlennogo proizvodstva*, (1): 104–118.

Zaigraev, G. 1985. *Sotsiologicheskie issledovaniia* (4): 47–54.

GORBACHEV AND
THE SOVIET NATIONALITY PROBLEM

Paul A. Goble

Mikhail Gorbachev's "nationality problem" is at once different and more serious than those faced by his predecessors. It is different because of the enormous social, economic, and political changes that have transformed the role of nationality in Soviet life since the death of Stalin. And it is more serious because of Gorbachev himself, his immediate political needs, and his long-term policy goals, all of which pose a challenge to the status of Soviet ethnic communities. In this essay, I want to explore each of the elements in this complex equation and then to suggest some of the possible outcomes for the nationalities and for Gorbachev himself.

The new face of the Soviet nationalities

In the past, Western students of the Soviet nationality problem have often limited themselves to an examination of only those issues that Moscow has defined as being part of it, such as language, culture, and loyalty. As a result of this narrow view, we have sometimes failed to see how much the Soviet nationalities have been transformed, how issues that used to be crucial have declined in importance, and how completely new ones have emerged. Part of the reason for this has been the pattern of Soviet data—a great deal on some subjects but very little or none about many others. But part of it lies in our general failure to treat Soviet nationality problems in a comparative perspective, to draw on

Paul A. Goble is Special Assistant for Soviet Nationality Affairs in the State Department's Bureau of Intelligence and Research. The views expressed in this paper are his own and not necessarily those of the Department or the U.S. Government.

the insights of social science literature concerning both colonial and ethnic politics. Now, under Gorbachev, our first excuse has been largely removed as a result of the unprecedented publication of various kinds of data. Consequently, we need to expand our vision on a variety of fronts.

As a contribution to this effort, I want to do three things in this section. First, I want to consider changes over the last generation in the systemic meaning of nationality. Here I will examine changes in the source of national identity, in the importance of nationality for Soviet citizens as a whole, and in its relevance for official behavior. Second, I want to examine objective changes in the nationalities themselves, particularly those social, economic, and political developments that I believe have transformed Moscow's nationality problem. And third, I want to trace changes in attitudes and expectations among Soviet citizens of different nationalities and to consider their impact on behavior under different levels of coercion.

The new meaning of nationality

Since the death of Stalin, there have been three major changes in the meaning of nationality in the USSR: a change in its primary source, a change in its importance for individuals, and a change in its impact on the system.

The most dramatic change has been in the primary source of national identity and nationalism. Traditionally, Soviet writers have defined these as *perezhitki*, "survivals of the past," destined to be mechanically overcome in the course of economic and political development. They have followed the declines in popular attachment to particular traditions and the rise in various indicators of Sovietization and claimed to see in these figures a vindication of their views. Curiously, many Western scholars have accepted this definition, though not the same conclusion. Instead, they have gathered evidence of the continued vitality of certain folk traditions and of popular resistance to Sovietization.

This debate is not so much wrong as it is sterile, for it does not help us to understand the often contradictory quality of ethnic development in the USSR. Further, it detracts attention from a new and more important source of national identity and nationalism there. That is the intense competition for jobs and resources among elites of various national groups rather than simple attachment to tradition. As Arutiunian and other Soviet ethnosociologists have shown, this kind of national identity and sensitivity arises precisely among those groups that are the most mobilized and Sovietized and on whom Moscow has counted the most. Further, these scholars have argued, as social development proceeds and these elites expand in size, this kind of national identity is likely to intensify even as the older type, found largely among the peasants and based on a xenophobic attachment to tradition, ebbs. The unintended consequence of the success of Soviet social policies, this kind of national identification is likely to prove an ever greater problem for the authorities in Moscow.

Adopting a comparative perspective, we can make two further points. First, as development proceeds, the possibilities that this form of national identity will be exacerbated dramatically increase—especially if a new leader tries to challenge what the national elites have come to view as their just desserts. And second, the two kinds of national identity are not entirely distinct. Ethnicity of all kinds has certain objective referents. Under conditions of high coercion and control, there is little chance that the two can ever link up and mobilize against the central authorities for any policy goal. But as coercion and control decline, the possibilities for such link-ups increase, especially under conditions of economic stagnation and direct challenges to what have come to be seen as national prerogatives by both groups. In looking at the nationality situation in the USSR, we should not forget that the leaders of successful ethnic political challenges and anticolonial movements have almost always come not from the most backward but from the most assimilated groups. Nor of course should we forget that these leaders have had to be able to tap the sentiments of the mass groups.

If changes in the source of ethnic identity point toward one set of conclusions, the change in the importance of nationality for individuals points toward quite another. Under totalitarian conditions, the basic division in society is between the few who have the power and the many atomized citizenry who do not. Ethnic consciousness—like all other identities based on normal societal divisions—is, in such circumstances, of distinctly secondary importance.[1] As the totalitarian regime decays or seeks to modify itself, however, ethnic consciousness increases in importance as both a source of meaning in everyday life and a personal refuge against the general dehumanization accompanying forced-march industrialization.

But it is not the only group identity to increase in importance at that time: class, professional group, region, all these and more now exert a pull on the individual. This proliferation of possible—or better, available—identities has important consequences for both the individual and the regime. For the individual, it may lead to a sense of confusion. As the hero of one recent Uzbek novel put it, he constantly felt like a *matrëshka* doll that others were assembling and disassembling almost at will. As a result, he was constantly unsure of just who he really was.[2] Depending on circumstances, this juggling of identities may lead to an intensification or weakening of national identity both in specific circumstances and over time. Alternatively, it may convert it into something purely instrumental, but no less powerful; a recent cartoon from Uzbekistan, showing girls in mini-skirts being photographed behind a board portraying them in traditional dress, makes that point.[3]

For the regime, the appearance of multiple identities dictates a strategy. As I have argued elsewhere,[4] the Soviet authorities must so structure environments that national identity does not dominate either identification choices or behavior in crucial situations. In the past, the disproportion between the resources of the state and those of the nationalities was so great that the regime had little difficulty in achieving its goal. That continues to be true. For example, when the authorities were faced with a nationalist challenge in Kazakhstan in December 1986, they quickly played up class divisions within the Kazakh community to undercut and contain that challenge. Alternatively, whenever the regime wants to shore up its authority with the Russians or other Slavic groups, it can do so by playing on fears about the foreign threat to the Soviet Union, thus justifying both repression and sacrifice. Given the recent loosening in certain areas, however, the regime's ability to structure all environments has certainly declined, at least at the margins. As a result, for at least some individuals in some circumstances, the regime may not be able to maintain its past level of success unless it is somehow able to deploy more economic resources than it is likely to have or more coercion than it may want, given other goals.

And third, there has been a major change in the accepted impact of nationality in the system. Following the revolution, the Soviet government made a commitment to end the radical inequalities then existing among the national groups. To reach this goal, Moscow instituted both massive transfer payments from the more developed regions to the less developed ones and an affirmative action system designed to place non-Russians in at least the most visible if not the most powerful positions at the republic and local level. Neither of these policies, of course, was unselfish: Moscow clearly hoped for both expanded economic growth and better integration of the non-Russian nationalities; but to a remarkable extent, they worked—and to the benefit of the non-Russian nationalities.

However, as the inequalities were reduced and in certain areas even reversed, many Russians came to the conclusion that what had appeared to be reasonable affirmative action for the non-Russians was in fact unreasonable reverse discrimination against themselves. Their anger, which surfaced increasingly often in the 1960s, '70s, and '80s, was only increased by the decline of their own region, their direct experience in non-Russian regions, the attitude of many non-Russians that this form of affirmative action was theirs by right, and the findings of many economists that past investment in the periphery had combined with inefficient, even corrupt republic-level management to slow down the country's rate of economic growth. As a result, many Russian officials have been seeking to reduce the importance of nationality in the system both for instrumental reasons and as a way of enhancing their own clout.

Their efforts have elicited the expected response in the republics, where local elites have tried to maximize the importance of nationality within their republics and to maintain its importance in all-union decision making. By the end of the Brezhnev era, they were hugely successful in the first case and almost equally successful at the center. As recent exposés of the situation in Kazakhstan under Kunaev have made clear, republic elites were able at that time to pack universities with professors and students of the indigenous nationality and to take control of an ever greater number of levers of economic and political power.[5] They were able to advance six republic first secretaries into the Politburo, their greatest level of representation there ever, and even to make common cause at the Twenty-sixth CPSU Congress in 1981. As a result, the earlier consensus on the proper role of nationality in the Soviet political system was largely shattered, exacerbating the sensitivities of both Russians and non-Russians and leaving to Brezhnev's successors an ethnic problem without precedent.

Objective changes in the nationalities themselves

The three changes just described both inform and reflect the social, economic, and political developments to be considered now. Before doing that, however, I want to make a general comment about the two biggest pitfalls in the current study of Soviet nationalities: excessive stress on complexity and excessive interest in the exotic. The Soviets regularly advertise that there are more than 100 nationalities in the USSR. While this is true, it is a fact that tends to distort the real situation by trivializing the importance of both the larger nationalities and the major divisions within and among them. In fact, the overwhelming majority of these groups are very small. Of those listed in the 1979 census, 43 numbered under 100,000 each; and 30 more between 100,000 and a million. Together, these 73 formed less than 3 percent of the population. While interesting and occasionally instructive—sometimes the Soviets discuss general nationality problems only in the context of these small, politically marginal groups—they cannot be said to constitute the basic pattern of the nationality scene today.

That is made up of the 22 largest nationalities numbering a million or more each. Fifteen of these—including 13 of the 14 largest—have their own union republics within the federal system and constitute over 90 percent of the population. Because of their importance and because most of the available data are collected along republic nationality lines, these 15 and the even larger cultural groups into which they fall are my subject here.

The other trap in the study of nationalities—overattention to the exotic aspects of the subject—must also be avoided. Many of our favored sources—ethnographers and antireligious specialists—have a vested interest in the unusual or unique; and many of us find their reports far more intrinsically interesting and entertaining than sociological studies and census reports. Unfortunately, the importance of these unique features is often much less than we suppose and that of the surveys and census tracts rather more, as any reflection about our own society would confirm. Take but one obvious example: sufism, the mystical strain within Soviet Islam. Many in the West have been impressed by these groups as a potential threat to Soviet power. If that is so, however, how is one to explain the fact that the latest issue of the Daghestan party journal publishes a list of the names, addresses, and activities of such groups over the last two decades?[6] If they were as dangerous as some have assumed, no doubt the KGB would already have made its move.

Of the many social changes that have occurred among the Soviet nationalities over the last generation, I want to focus on three: demographic shifts, changes in educational attainment and language use, and the emergence of new, non-Russian elites. The basic demographic

Table 1

Changing Relative Size of Slavic and Muslim Republic Nationalities, 1959–1989 (as percentage of total population)

	Slavic Nationalities	Muslim Nationalities
1959	76.2	7.7
1970	74.0	9.9
1979	72.2	12.0
1989 (est.)	68.4	13.7

Source: "Bilim zhane engbek," *Kazak* 11 (1986), pp. 31–33.

changes are the most well known. They show a major shift away from the traditional Slavic groups (Russians, Ukrainians, and Belorussians) to the traditionally "Muslim" nationalities (Uzbek, Azerbaijani, Kirghiz, Kazakh, and Tajik) (Table 1). Because these numbers did not include non–republic-level nationalities, they slightly understate the extent of the shift. Even so, it is dramatic: from 10 to 1 Slavic dominance in 1959 to only 5 to 1 thirty years later, with the Russians dropping to an estimated 50 percent of the population in 1989. While these changes would not translate directly into political changes even in a democratic society, they nevertheless have had a profound political and psychological impact on both groups, frightening the one and encouraging the other.

Behind this global change are major and well-known divergences in expected and actual family size, in short, the birthrate. Indeed, according to one Soviet study, family size is the only major social variable where the coefficient of variation increased rather than fell between 1959 and 1979.[7] Part of this reflects the impact of urbanization on the Slavs and improved medical services for the Muslims; but even after these are factored out, major differences in family size preferences remain. This has forced Soviet specialists to conclude that their earlier mechanical models of the demographic transition are inadequate and that the Islamic population "boom" is likely to continue, albeit at reduced rates, well into the future.[8] Indeed, at least one Kazakh demographer has suggested that the Muslim nationalities will account for over 50 percent of Soviet population growth during the entire next century.[9]

Compounding the effects of this have been changes in migration

Table 2

**Percentage of the Indigenous Population in the
Total Population of Union Republics, 1959 and 1979**

Republic	1959	1979	Republic	1959	1979
RSFSR	83.2	82.6	Lithuania	79.6	80.0
Ukraine	76.9	73.5	Latvia	62.0	53.7
Belorussia	81.6	77.5	Kirghizia	41.8	48.2
Uzbekistan	62.2	69.0	Turkmenistan	61.5	68.5
Kazakhstan	30.3	36.2	Tajikistan	53.1	58.8
Georgia	65.0	70.0	Armenia	88.1	90.8
Azerbaijan	67.9	78.4	Estonia	74.9	64.9

Source: Arutiunian, Iu. V. and Bromlei, Iu., eds., *Sotsial'no-kul'turnyi oblik Sovetskikh natsii* (Moscow, 1986), pp. 27–28.

patterns, for the latter have dramatically changed the extent of ethnic mixing, or ''mosaicness,'' in the Soviet republics (see Table 2). The republics fall into three groups:

—those where migration has reduced the percentage of the titular nationality (RSFSR, Latvia, Estonia, and more recently Armenia);

—those where migration has had little or no effect (Ukraine, Belorussia, and Lithuania); and

—those where migration patterns have combined with population growth to increase the concentration of the titular nationality (Georgia, Moldavia, and all ''Muslim'' nationality republics).

The third group divides into two parts: those republics—Moldavia, Kazakhstan, and Uzbekistan—where the Russian influx continues but is smaller than its level in the population; and all others—where the Russians are suffering a net loss and moving out.[10] Significantly, this means that non-Russians now have at least a plurality in all republics and large majorities in most. Even in Kazakhstan, the Kazakhs now outnumber the Russians, a fact announced just before the Alma-Ata riots and one that made the imposition of an ethnic Russian first secretary especially galling.[11]

Migration patterns also were behind changes in the ethnic mix in the republic capitals. During the 1970s, the share of the indigenous nationality increased in Minsk, Kishinev, Vilnius, Tbilisi, Baku, Alma-Ata, Frunze, Dushanbe, and Ashkhabad; in several cases, including Dushanbe and Baku, this was largely because of the outflow of Russians. In three capitals (Riga, Erevan, and Tallin), however, migration con-

Table 3

Average Monthly Pay in Agriculture as a Percentage of Pay in Industry, 1970–1980, by Republic

Republic	1970	1980	Republic	1970	1980
USSR	75.8	80.5	Lithuania	64.5	78.6
RSFSR	71.9	80.5	Latvia	82.3	91.3
Ukraine	72.8	82.8	Kirghizia	68.5	74.3
Belorussia	63.8	75.3	Tajikistan	82.5	92.7
Uzbekistan	79.2	91.6	Armenia	67.6	69.0
Georgia	62.8	65.6	Turkmenistan	93.3	87.1
Azerbaijan	64.8	84.4	Estonia	86.2	94.6

Source: N. A. Aitov, *Sotsial'noe razvitie regionov* (Moscow, 1985), p. 134.

formed to the earlier pattern and had the opposite effect.[12] This too affected local attitudes, as we shall see below.

A third demographic variable on which the nationalities continued to diverge was urbanization. While the general correlation of variability on this indicator fell between 1959 and 1979,[13] major differences remained. This was especially true in Central Asia, where rural youth, even when well trained, showed little inclination to move to their own cities, let alone to labor-short Slavic regions. As one sociologist complained, labor has been flowing in the wrong direction from an economic point of view since the 1950s;[14] that is, since economic incentives had to replace coercion as the steering mechanism.

Not content with an ethnic explanation, Soviet scholars have found that Soviet policy itself is largely to blame. As a result of its efforts to improve rural pay and living conditions, Moscow has created a situation in which rural Central Asians have very little incentive to move. The impact of these pay differentials is reinforced by differences in quality of life, availability of housing, and, importantly, opportunities in the second economy.[15]

The second major change has been in language-use patterns and educational attainment levels. Moscow has always promoted Russian bilingualism among its non-Russian population for both political and practical reasons. As a result of the demographic changes outlined above and their impact on both the economy and the military, it has redoubled its efforts in the last decade. And it has achieved some notable successes: between 1970 and 1979, the percentage of non-

Table 4

**Years of Schooling of Republic Nationalities,
1959–1979 (*per capita* 10 years of age and above)**

Nationality	1959	1970	1979
Russians	5.2	6.4	7.8
Ukrainians	4.9	6.0	7.4
Belorussians	4.6	5.8	7.2
Uzbeks	4.0	5.3	6.3
Kazakhs	3.9	5.3	6.3
Georgians	5.9	7.2	8.7
Azerbaijanis	4.6	4.9	7.5
Moldavians	3.6	4.8	6.5
Latvians	5.6	6.3	7.5
Kirghiz	4.0	5.1	6.9
Tajiks	4.0	5.3	7.1
Armenians	5.6	6.5	8.4
Turkmens	4.3	5.4	7.1
Estonians	5.6	6.5	7.5
Lithuanians	3.9	5.3	6.9

Source: Sotsial'no-kul'turnyi oblik . . . , p. 214.

Russians who claimed Russian as either a native or second language rose from 48.9 to 62.2 percent. Even if the latter figure is exaggerated—and Soviet demographers now regularly concede that it is—such a level is impressive; but it has brought the Soviet authorities little peace:

—First of all, it has not been even throughout the USSR. Among Estonians, for example, the percentage claiming knowledge of Russian actually dropped during the 1970s. And as ethnic mixing declines, that pattern may be repeated elsewhere.

—Second, Russian-language knowledge has remained especially low among draft-age Central Asians, forcing the military authorities to devote a disproportionate amount of time to instruction in the language of command.

—And third and most critical from Moscow's point of view, acquisition of Russian has not contributed to significant reidentification among union-republic nationalities. (The major exception consists of Ukrainians, and then only among those living outside the Ukraine.)[16]

Instead, the rise in Russian-language knowledge has made it more likely that non-Russians can and will compete with Russians for jobs and resources and that their national identities will be intensified and

Table 5

**Applicants for Higher School Admission
(number per 100 places, by republic)**

Georgia	412	Belorussia	232
Azerbaijan	406	Moldavia	217
Turkmenistan	302	Ukraine	208
Armenia	299	RSFSR	202
Uzbekistan	293	Latvia	188
Kirghizia	287	Lithuania	184
Tajikistan	281	Estonia	153
Kazakhstan	244		

Source: G. V. Makartsev and V. T. Lisovskii, *Sovremennyi student* (Tbilisi, 1982), p. 122.

national sensitivities exacerbated in the process. The most impressive and in some ways surprising evidence of this is to be found in the resurgence of national identification and pride among Russian-speaking Belorussians.

In education, there have also been great changes at all levels. Non-Russians have made enormous gains in recent years as Table 4 shows, and the correlation of variation on educational attainment among republic nationalities has dropped by nearly 50 percent.[17] As a result, the republics have an increasingly well-educated but not always well-employed workforce, a fact confirmed by the 1985 minicensus[18] and, as we shall see, not an unmixed blessing.

Most dramatic of all have been the changes at the higher and specialized secondary levels. Until the 1950s, these levels were dominated by Slavic and other European nationalities such as the Jews. Then, under Khrushchev, things began to change. By 1960–61, the local nationalities were overrepresented in the higher schools in Kazakhstan, Georgia, and Estonia; by 1970–71, this was true in the majority of republics. Moreover, the disproportions were increasing.[19] And the pressure for even greater indigenous enrollment remained high throughout the 1970s, a time when all-union rates were generally declining because of trends among the Slavic groups (see Table 5).[20]

Part of this pattern reflects simple demographics—where birthrates are low, application pressure is likely to be low as well—but part of it is the product of differences in national values. Recent Soviet polls show that aspirations for higher education are greater among republic nation-

Table 6

Ratio of Higher School Students to Technicum Students by Nationality in Two Republics

Estonia	
Estonians	1.2
Russians	.8
Georgia	
Georgians	1.2
Russians	.7

Source: Sotsial'no-kul'turnyi oblik . . . , p. 92.

alities without a working-class tradition than they are among nationalities with one. This pattern was confirmed by a recent poll of unskilled workers in Uzbekistan. It showed that 72 percent of the Uzbeks as against only 57 percent of the Russians wanted their children to acquire a higher education.[21]

This pattern has several obvious consequences that will be considered below in the sections on elites and popular attitudes. One, however, needs to be mentioned here: the continued Russian/Slavic dominance in technical training schools. This becomes obvious when one compares higher school enrollment to technicum enrollment by nationality (see Table 6). Such a pattern has two potentially significant consequences. First, it is likely to exacerbate ethnic tensions among both students and graduates seeking work. And second, it adds a powerful ethnic dimension to any effort to bring the educational system more closely in line with the economy's technical requirements.

These educational developments have already had a major impact on both the size and the structure of non-Russian elites. In many republics, the large university enrollments mean that graduates have a hard time finding a position and must increasingly take jobs beneath the level of their qualifications. In Estonia, for example, only 70 percent of the higher school trained specialists could find work for which they were qualified in 1980.[22] In such jobs, they more often find themselves competing with less well-trained but fully qualified Russians.

More important, though, are changes in the structure of the elite itself and in the supply and demand situation in each sector. In most republics, the two parts of the intelligentsia traditionally dominated by the local nationalities—the administrative-political elite and the creative intelligentsia—are declining relatively and in some cases even absolutely while the two parts of it most often dominated by Russians or other outsiders—economic management and scientific cadres—have expanded. As in the case of the elite as a whole, in each of these areas there is a serious gap between the supply of new graduates and the demand for their services.

Most striking is the situation in republic-level creative intelligentsias. Traditionally the domain of non-Russian intellectuals, these groups expanded until the early 1970s, when Moscow concluded that non-Russian writers and other creative types were overrepresented relative to Russian ones and announced that technical developments such as radio, television, and mass publishing had made further growth not only unnecessary but undesirable.[23] This cap has not been observed everywhere, but it has tended to increase competition for places, thus giving the local authorities and Moscow an additional means of control over them and increasing tensions within artistic elites.

Far more interesting, however, is the changing relationship between the Slavic-dominated economic elites and the local-dominated (at least numerically) political-administrative elite. With economic development, there has been a secular trend toward the growth of the former relative to the latter. In 1939, the ratio between the two was 3.6 to 1 for the country as a whole; by 1979, it had risen to 5 to 1. This trend obviously works to the disadvantage of the formerly less well-educated non-Russians who could more easily fill political than technical positions, and by default sets up a more intense competition in the two areas dominated by Slavs. Seeing this, some republic elites sought to keep the ratio down by expanding the size of the political elite into which they could place their co-nationals. This pattern was especially marked in the 1970s. During that period, Kazakhstan and Kirghizia maintained administrative-political elites that were twice as large relative to their economic elites as the all-union pattern.[24] Such bloated bureaucracies obviously make tempting targets for any Soviet leader committed to increasing economic efficiency; but as recent events in Alma-Ata attest, they can be directly attacked only at a very high price.

Let us now turn briefly to the economic and political changes and their impact on the nationalities. Because each of these has been touched on in passing above, they need only be briefly summarized here. Concerning economic development, three main points:

—Economic growth has not eliminated the basic divisions between agricultural and industrial regions and hence between the average *per capita* incomes in the republics.[25]

—Differences in rates both within and between regions have generated enormous differences in expectations and in the general tendency to invest competition with ethnic meaning. Further, the general economic slowdown has exacerbated these tendencies.

—The movements of both capital and labor have become less rational over time as a result of political considerations on the one hand and extra-economic concerns and preferences on the other.

Together, these have contributed to significant differences in productivity growth,[26] and hence to increased conflict over investment patterns.

The major political changes may be summarized equally briefly. Throughout the post-Stalin period, non-Russian representation in the party became more proportional, with the Slavic dominance reduced but not yet eliminated.[27] But the major changes in the last generation concerned non-Russian control over their own republics and non-Russian representation at the center, especially during the Brezhnev era. As a result of Brezhnev's approach to cadres, non-Russian republic leaders were able to pack their bureaucracies with their own people and to create entrenched political machines. While overall control remained in Slavic hands through the key second secretary position, the locals gained so much power and self-confidence that many Russians living in the republics felt their own positions threatened. (That was the impetus behind Brezhnev's 1981 call for better protection of the interests of nonindigenous nationalities.) At the same time, as we have already seen, non-Russian representation rose to new highs at the center. Six republic first secretaries were on the Politburo near the end of the Brezhnev period, but they did not crack either the Central Committee secretariat or most of the major ministries. This growth in representation, however, clearly created expectations that were destined to remain unrealized.

Changes in attitudes, expectations, and attachments

For any complete assessment of ethnic politics, attitudes, expectations, and attachments are what matter most; but under Soviet conditions, they are precisely the most difficult to discover. Because we cannot do survey research in the USSR itself and because we could not use any results so obtained with much confidence if we were permitted to do so, we have typically relied on a variety of indirect measures: interviews with émigrés and Soviets traveling abroad, Soviet literature, and Soviet media commentaries. All have been useful, but each has its particular limitations—especially on sensitive subjects like ethnic attitudes and political loyalties.

Now the Soviets have provided an alternative source of information for these most interesting questions: their own polls of several thousand Soviet citizens in five different republics. Conducted over the last twenty years, these samplings are not without problems. We must assume that at least some of the time the pollsters were told—or at least they recorded—what they wanted to hear. At the same time, the scholars involved were both careful and methodologically sophisticated, and their indirect approach to some of these questions—they obviously have their own reasons for this, too—gives one greater confidence in their findings.[28] Consequently, in this section, I want to use their data to explore changes in ethnic attitudes, expectations, and attachments.

One of the most interesting and important questions concerns an individual's relative attachment to the Soviet Union and to his own nationality and republic. Unfortunately, we have only the most indirect evidence on this point. In the five-republic study, citizens were asked "What do you consider your motherland [rodina]—the country as a whole, the republic in which you live, the republic of your own nationality, or something else?" The overwhelming majority of every national group listed as their motherland both the USSR and the republic of their own nationality. In the RSFSR and Uzbekistan, for example, more than three-quarters of the respective nationalities listed the USSR as their motherland, with the other quarter naming the republic of their own nationality. In Moldavia, a republic that until World War II had been part of Romania, the same percentages held. Among groups living outside their own republic or among minorities lacking a republic of their own, the picture is only slightly different: 60 percent of Armenians, Azerbaijanis, and Ossetians living in Georgia named the USSR as their motherland; 25 percent of them named Georgia; and 15 percent named their home ethnic territory.[29]

While these data are far from perfect or complete, they do suggest two important conclusions. First, the overwhelming majority of non-Russians do identify themselves as Soviet citizens. This in turn suggests that under normal conditions, nationality politics in the USSR will be played out as a variant of within-system ethnic politics rather than system-challenging colonial politics. And second, most of them also have a strong attachment to the republic of their own nationality and to the one in which they live—increasingly the same for most groups. This in turn points up the strength of republics as an expression of national identity and of the identities themselves. Although the data available do not permit a definitive judgment, both these attachments— to the USSR and to the republics—have undoubtedly strengthened over time.

The second major finding of these polls concerns the intensification of national identity among union-republic nationalities. So strong is this trend that it is now enshrined in the party's ideological formula about national development under socialism. The polls suggest two reasons for this intensification of feeling. First is its important contribution to a sense of efficacy and the satisfaction of a variety of psychological needs. As the republics increased in importance in the 1960s and 1970s and as local elites pushed their own people forward, non-Russian groups had an expanded sense that they had an impact on their social environment via their membership in these groups. During the same period, Russians appear to have dropped on these same measures, perhaps because of the special status of the RSFSR.[30] The second reason for the intensification of national identity is already familiar: competition for jobs and resources.[31] As more non-Russians became qualified for jobs held by Russians, both groups have tended to invest the situation with ethnic meaning, especially in the case of failure. Not surprisingly, given their relative decline, Russians tend to do so even more than other groups. Important, too, for understanding what happened in Alma-Ata, such competition and its product, increased ethnic sensitivity, are more common in republic capitals than anywhere else in the Soviet Union.[32]

And the third major finding, which flows from the second, concerns attitudes toward other national groups. The Soviet research team found that hostility of this kind ranged from 2 to 10 percent across all republic-level nationalities and that these levels had remained virtually constant throughout the Brezhnev period.[33] This general finding, however, obscures two trends pointing in opposite directions. On the one hand, all studies agree, Soviet citizens generally are increasingly well disposed toward working in multinational collectives. On the other, they remain attached—and in some cases are becoming more attached—to their own national traditions and values in the most intimate spheres of life and are openly hostile to any intervention designed to supplant

---

Table 7

**Value Orientations of Uzbeks and Russians
(ranked by percentage mentioning each value)**

Russians	Uzbeks
Family 85	Family 72
Interesting work 78	Respect of one's fellows 59
Material well-being 74	A peaceful life 54
Respect of one's fellows 70	Material well-being 49
A peaceful life 25	Interesting work 45

Source: Sotsial'no-kul'turnyi oblik . . . , p. 251.

---

these with values drawn from another culture.

Expectations about the future also play an important role in defining national attitudes. In general, there has been a revolution of rising expectations created among most non-Russian groups. Those nationalities—the Central Asians, especially—that have advanced the farthest fastest have the most optimism about the future, and those that have suffered relative decline—the Slavs and the Balts—have the least. As a result, the first group is more likely to feel positive about itself, while the second is more likely to feel negative about others.[34] A corollary of this, explicitly drawn by the Soviet researchers, is that a general slowdown will tend to exacerbate national feelings in both groups while a major expansion will improve them[35]—a conclusion that should surprise no one familiar with ethnic politics elsewhere.

These surveys also tapped national differences in cultural preferences and attachment to the past traditions of the five national groups. While much attention has been given to these in the West, many factors of this kind emerge as major issues only when the regime launches a drive for ideological purity. The three issues to be considered here, however, have a major and continuing impact on the regime's ability to reach and motivate the population.

First, there are major differences in what motivates people. As Table 7 shows, Russians are far more influenced by economic considerations than are Uzbeks. Such a pattern makes it very difficult to achieve desired results through the use of economic stimuli alone.

Second, there are even larger differences among union-republic nationalities in how people choose to spend their free time. Some groups are thus clearly easier for the regime to reach than are others.

Table 8

Preferred Literary Themes among Urban Residents of Five Republics (rank-ordered according to expressed interest among those polled)

Nationality	Themes
Russians	1. About the war 2. About love and friendship 3. Adventure stories 4. About the past of one's own people 5. Sociopolitical topics 6. Psychological books 7. By specialty
Uzbeks	1. About love and friendship 2. About the past of one's own people 3. About the war 4. Adventure stories 5. By specialty 6. Psychological books 7. Sociopolitical topics
Georgians	1. About the war 2. About the past of one's own people 3. By specialty 4. Psychological books 5. Sociopolitical topics
Moldavians	1. About the war 2. About love and friendship 3. Adventure stories 4. Sociopolitical topics 5. Psychological books 6. About the past of one's own people 7. By specialty
Estonians	1. Adventure stories 2. Psychological books 3. About the past of one's own people 4. About love and friendship 5. About the war 6. By specialty 7. Sociopolitical topics

Source: Sotsial'no-kul'turnyi oblik . . . , p. 231.

Reading, for example, is a far more frequent and valued activity among urban Russians, Georgians, and Estonians than it is among urban Moldavians and Uzbeks. On the other hand, television is far more significant for rural Russians and Moldavians than for any other nationality, urban or rural. While much of the variance can be explained by access or boredom, it cannot be ignored by the authorities.[36]

Third, reflecting national traditions, there are significant differences in popular interest in the type of reading and theatre repertoires preferred. A recent study of literary preferences showed major differences in the level of interest in books about the war as against those about the past of one's own people, a surrogate measure of people's attitudes toward Soviet values and toward national ones (see Table 8).

A study of theatre repertoires throughout the USSR found that the republics fall into seven groups according to the rank order of Russian, national, other non-Russian, and foreign plays performed:

1. National and then Russian: Ukraine, Uzbekistan, Kazakhstan, Kirghizia, and Turkmenistan;

2. National and then foreign: RSFSR and Latvia;

3. Foreign and then national: Estonia and Lithuania;

4. National, then those of other non-Russians, and Russian: Azerbaijan;

5. National, then foreign and Russian: Georgia and Armenia;

6. Russian and then national: Tajikistan; and

7. Russian, then national and foreign: Belorussia.[37]

This pattern of attachment to national traditions and resistance to Russian-laden Sovietization is too obvious to require comment. It does highlight, however, the fact that Moscow can pursue a rigidly uniform cultural policy only at the price of nearly certain failure and much-exacerbated national sensitivities.

Gorbachev's approach to the nationalities

This complex nationality situation would have confronted any Soviet leader after Brezhnev; in fact, it now confronts Mikhail Gorbachev, and his response to it already appears very different from that of any of his predecessors. Gorbachev is the first Soviet leader since Lenin not to have served in a non-Russian republic at any point in his career, and he is the first ever not to have articulated a specific nationality policy shortly after coming to power. (I believe that that has a lot to do with what his intentions toward the nationalities really are.) Consequently, we have to discuss his approach to the nationalities in a very different way than we have done with past Soviet leaders. In this section, I want to do three things: first, consider Gorbachev the man, the experiences and attitudes that he acquired prior to becoming party leader; second, look briefly at the various policy initiatives he has undertaken since coming to power; and third, examine his immediate power-political needs and how these have brought him into conflict with the republics.

Gorbachev the man

When Gorbachev slipped during a June 1985 walkabout in Kiev and referred to the Soviet Union as "Russia," many non-Russians and Western observers immediately decided that they now had the measure of the man. Most concluded that the new party leader was a thorough-going Russian nationalist. They could not have been more wrong, but to understand why, we must examine his earlier career.

Gorbachev grew up and worked in Stavropol' krai, a region where nationality did not matter very much, and he absorbed that attitude. The area was overwhelmingly Russian, and hence national distinctions were not an issue. The only exception were the Karachai and Cherkess nationalities, two groups deported after the war and then allowed to return after the Twentieth Party Congress. As far as can be known, his attitude toward them was one of concern about possible deviation from the norm, but he does not appear to have been especially negative. In all of this, he is very typical of anyone with a background in a mono-ethnic environment.

Nor did he devote much attention to the nationalities question as he rose through the ranks. A search of his published writings and speeches prior to coming to power shows that he spoke about nationality issues rarely—no more than four times before December 1984. In that, too, he was not atypical of an RSFSR party leader.

Only at the December 1984 ideological conference did he reveal himself. He made three comments about the nationalities, all of which reflected his past:

—First, he called for zero-based budgeting, a direct challenge to the republics' role in the economy;

—Second, he treated the periphery in an undifferentiated way, not giving pride of place to the republics over the oblasts of the RSFSR; and

—Third, he appeared to call for an end to affirmative action, arguing that the selection of cadres in both Moscow and the republics should be conducted the same way—on merit and without favoritism.

Such an approach reflects the mind of a man who is both a committed Leninist and an economic rationalist and who has not thought much about nationality issues of any kind. But in a multinational environment, to ignore the equity claims of nationalities in the name of efficiency is to change the rules of the game and to tilt the board, intentionally or not, to the largest and dominant group—in this case, the Russians. There is no evidence that that is the animus of Gorbachev's policies, but that is likely to be their effect. Hence, the non-Russians in the leadership resisted his coming to power and the non-Russian elites in the republics took a defensive position once he was there.

Policy initiatives and policy debate

Since becoming general secretary, Gorbachev has been consistent with himself. As his specific moves are well known, I want only to comment on the three major areas in which his policies have affected the nationalities.

First, reflecting a new self-confidence in the stability of the country, Gorbachev has sought to remove minor irritants by allowing the Meskhetians—a small Turkic group deported from Georgia at the end of World War II—to return, for example, and to acknowledge past mistakes, at least to a limited degree. He has not been afraid to put people in office who will look the nationality problem in the face—such as the Siberian economist Aganbegian, and General Lizichev, the chief of the Soviet army's political administration—but he has required that they approach it from efficiency rather than equity grounds. If something will help achieve his goals, fine; if it will help only a particular nationality, then it is probably not on.

Second, in promoting economic reform, Gorbachev has sought to engineer transfer of industrial plant from the republics to the USSR,[38] regularly expressed hostility to the inefficiencies of bloated middle management, of which the republics are the outstanding examples, and instituted a change in the budget process so that specific projects rather than additions to what has already been done are the chief planning criterion. All of these have earned him the enmity of republic elites because they have cost the elites power without yet bringing them any benefits.

And third, he has promoted openness. With respect to the nationalities, this has had two important effects. First, it has made it possible for a variety of people to push views, reducing our ability to determine any line. For example, loosening in literature has allowed both Russian nationalists and Ukrainian nationalists to appear in print, generating support for their two positions but not necessarily indicating where Moscow wants to go. And second, it has exacerbated national sensitivities by raising the possibility that sensitive issues will be discussed sometime soon, allowing certain authors to push a variety of often nationalist-inspired ideas, and highlighting more than ever before just how different appear to be the controls on Russian and non-Russian writers. Because of the transformations detailed above, there are much larger attentive audiences than ever before.

Of course, not all of these outcomes depended on Gorbachev alone. There is much evidence that *de facto* second secretary Egor Ligachev played a hand, and his statements suggest that there is a far higher dose of Russian nationalism in his thinking than there is in Gorbachev's. Further, the debate preceding the adoption of the new party program highlighted tensions not only between Russians and non-Russians but among Moscow leaders in how to proceed.[39] These attitudes are obviously playing a major role behind the scenes.

Immediate political needs

The major thrust of Gorbachev's nationality policy is directed toward his immediate political needs. None of his policies will be adopted unless he can solidify his support at the center and none of them will be implemented if he confronts hostile political machines on the periphery. Consequently, Gorbachev must seek to break their power, putting his own men in charge, and ensuring that he can control the subordinate levels of the bureaucracy through them.

Every new Soviet leader faces this challenge, but Gorbachev's task is particularly difficult for two reasons. First, as we have seen, devolution of power had proceeded further than in the past. The republics had acquired real control and authority, and the local populations—especially the elites—had come to see them as their most important protector and representative. And in addition, because of what had happened under Brezhnev, they had even greater expectations for the future. Thus, any move, even the most cautious and circumspect, would have been resisted and resisted passionately. But the second reason is that with Gorbachev that could not be so. While he clearly is a master of bureaucratic politics, he not only does not understand ethnic feelings but acts in a way guaranteed to exacerbate them even if he does not intend to.

Two examples spring to mind. First, in contrast to earlier leaders since the death of Stalin, Gorbachev has leveled charges against non-Russian leaders such as corruption and attachment to religion—Islam is the outstanding example—that give the officials no place to retreat. In part, this is typical of a Leninist leader; but in part, it conveys a lack of imagination. And second, believing as he does that expertise and ability matter above all, Gorbachev has directly challenged the non-Russians by reducing their representation in the Politburo—now there is only one republic first secretary there—and putting Russians into traditionally non-Russian slots in Central Asia and elsewhere. Had he chosen local Russians or cadres of the indigenous nationality, prepared to cooperate with his program—and all the evidence suggests that such people would be numerous—he would have achieved far more. Instead, he attacked and the result was Alma-Ata.

Gorbachev's "nationality problem"

The December 1986 protests in Alma-Ata following the appointment of an ethnic Russian as Kazakhstan's party leader precisely reflect Gorbachev's "nationality problem." On the one hand, he felt compelled for political power and policy reasons to remove a holdover from the Brezhnev regime and to crack the Kazakh party machine. On the other, he faced a new kind of resistance: Kazakh elites prepared to go to the streets to defend their privileges as Kazakhs. While they quickly backed down—the disproportion in power is just too great—soon Gorbachev had to retreat as well.

At the January plenum, Gorbachev failed to secure the removal of Ukraine's Shcherbitskii; and following the plenum, he allowed to be elected as Belorussian first secretary a man who had pursued the classic Brezhnev-era rise, all within the Belorussian republic. Further, Gorbachev even felt compelled to say that he was for "proper representation" of all nationalities at the center as well as in the republics. What this may mean from a man who has reduced non-Russian representation in both places remains to be seen, but it is certainly a concession. In short, Kunaev may have lost; but the nationalities did not.

This same pattern of the absence of a nationality policy or at least of a sensitivity to nationality issues appears to be hindering Gorbachev in all areas of policy initiative. His stress on economic efficiency is facing resistance because of its implications for power relations; his loosening of controls on the media is raising many potentially explosive questions; and his efforts to revive ideological élan have so far fallen flat because he has not been able to deliver on his promises. In each case, many non-Russians will be with him; but the existence of a more mobilized and sensitized multinational population will mean that the contradictions inherent in his policies will be magnified and that his chances of achieving his goals will be less. Indeed, his ultimate choice may be to back down on the issues mentioned above or to use more coercion, either of which would constitute a major defeat for his policies if not for the man himself.

In this sense then, Gorbachev's "nationality problem" is more serious than those of his predecessors. Given the ethnic scene, his own personality and goals have made it so. Clearly, the nationalities do not threaten the integrity of the system, but they may threaten Gorbachev's policies and even career. To that extent, Gorbachev may now be learning what many students of that part of the world have long suspected: that a liberalized Russia might be possible but that a significantly liberalized Soviet Union is probably a contradiction in terms.

Notes

1. On this, see Conquest 1980 and Davies 1982.
2. Kadyrov 1984, 10.
3. The cartoon, from the Uzbek humor magazine *Mushtum*, was reprinted in *Krokodil* 13 (May 1982), 5.
4. Goble 1985.
5. *Izvestiia*, January 24, 1987, 3.
6. Makatov 1986.
7. Arutiunian 1985, 21–23.
8. Arutiunian and Bromlei 1986, 122–25.
9. "Bilim zhane engbek" 1986, 33.
10. Arutiunian and Bromlei 1986, 27–28.
11. "Bilim zhane engbek" 1986, 33.
12. Arutiunian and Bromlei 1986, 29.
13. Arutiunian 1985, 23.
14. *Sotsiologicheskie issledovaniia* 1981 (4): 9–11.
15. Greenslade 1986, 620–25.
16. Arutiunian and Bromlei 1986.
17. Arutiunian 1985, 23.
18. See monthly reports in *Vestnik statistiki* 1986 (7–11).
19. Arutiunian and Bromlei 1986, 81–89, 184–85.
20. See *ibid.*, where an all-Union decline of 290 to 220 applicants per 100 places for the period 1960–1979 is contrasted with significant increases in Azerbaijan (330 to 370), Tajikistan (230 to 290), and Turkmenistan (235 to 290) during the same interval.
21. *Ibid.*, 78.
22. *Ibid.*, 100, 81.
23. *Ibid.*, 300, 62–63. Perhaps as a result, non-Russians are now underrepresented in the higher arts schools in the republics (*ibid.*, 89).

24. *Ibid.*, 60–62. This pattern of overrepresentation holds even if economic development is held constant. That is not the case for the three other republics—Tajikistan, Turkmenistan, and Moldavia—where the political-administrative elite remains relatively larger than the all-Union average.

25. *Narodnoe khoziaistvo* 1982, 469.

26. Aitov 1985, 35.

27. Arutiunian and Bromlei 1986, 244.

28. The findings of these polls are summarized in Arutiunian *et al.* 1972; *Sotsiologicheskie ocherki . . .* 1979; Arutiunian *et al.* 1980; and Arutiunian and Bromlei 1986. On the methodology employed, see especially Arutiunian *et al.* 1984.

29. Arutiunian and Bromlei 1986, 243.

30. *Ibid.*, 250, 136.

31. *Ibid.*, 392–406.

32. *Ibid.*, 395.

33. *Ibid.*, 358.

34. *Ibid.*, 365–66.

35. *Ibid.*, 378, 99–100.

36. *Ibid.*, 227.

37. *Ibid.*, 199.

38. *Pravda*, April 30, 1985.

39. For specifics, see Goble 1986a, 1; and Goble 1986b, 1–5.

Bibliography

Aitov, N. A. 1985. *Sotsial'noe razvitie regionov*. Moscow.

Arutiunian, Iu. V. 1985. "Sotsial'no-kul'turnaia obshchnost' sovetskikh natsii." In: *Natsiia i kul'tura*. Tallin.

Arutiunian, Iu. V. and Bromlei, Iu., eds. 1986. *Sotsial'no-kul'turnyi oblik Sovetskikh natsii*. Moscow.

Arutiunian, Iu. V. *et al.* 1972. *Sotsial'noe i natsional'noe*. Moscow.

———. 1980. *Opyt etnosotsiologicheskogo issledovaniia obraza zhizni (po materialam Moldavskoi SSR)*. Moscow.

———. 1984. *Etnosotsiologiia: tseli, metodi i nekotorye rezul'taty issledovaniia*. Moscow.

"Bilim zhane engbek." *Kazak* 11, 1986.

Conquest, Robert. 1980. *We and They*. London.

Davies, Christie. 1982. "Ethnic Jokes, Moral Values and Social Boundaries," *British Journal of Sociology* 33(3) (September).

Goble, Paul A. 1985. "Managing the Multinational USSR," *Problems of Communism* (July-August), 79–83.

———. 1986a. "Gorbachev's Nationality Policy Takes Shape." *Soviet Nationalities Survey* (10).

———. 1986b. "Nationality Tensions Reflected in New Party Program." *Soviet Nationalities Survey* (11).

Greenslade, Gertrude Shroeder. 1986. "Regional Dimensions of the Legal Private Economy in the USSR." National Council for Soviet and East European Research.

Kadyrov, Pirimkul. 1984. *Almaznyi poias*. Moscow.

Makartsev, G. V. and Lisovskii, V. T. 1982. *Sovremennyi student*. Tbilisi.

Makatov, I. 1986. "V ushcherb interesam obshchestva i lichnosti." *Sovetskii Dagestan* (6): 37–44.

Narodnoe khoziaistvo SSSR 1922–1982. 1982. Moscow.

Sotsiologicheskie ocherki o Sovetskoi Estonii 1979. Tallin.

GLASNOST' AND SOVIET CULTURE

Anthony Olcott

Signs of change

Ever since the dark days of the Zhdanovshchina, Soviet culture has been engaged in a painful uphill climb toward something resembling freedom of expression. Beginning from a Stalinist world in which every character on every printed page had, on pain of severe penalty, to adhere to a Party line, this trek has been both slow and erratic. It has been marked by the publication of works that upon appearance seemed exciting but now seem hopelessly turgid, and it has been beset with frequent reversals, such as the *Doctor Zhivago* and Solzhenitsyn crackdowns. Nevertheless, for all the slowness and all the reversals, Soviet culture has shown a steady movement toward greater license for artists to express their individual visions. Suddenly, however, the changes made by M. S. Gorbachev, particularly his introduction of *glasnost'*, have significantly widened the straits of the permitted, to such a degree that it might be possible to argue that the USSR has achieved, if not freedom of expression, then a close approximation of it.

For example, as recently as 1984, possession of works by Vladimir Nabokov was, if not by itself sufficient reason, damning enough to be one of the reasons the Leningrad translator, Orientalist, and book-speculator Mikhail Meilakh was sent to prison.[1] Now, a Soviet magazine, *64*, has published a short excerpt from Nabokov's memoirs, and the editor of *Moskva*, Mikhail Alekseev, has announced that "the time has come to return Nabokov to his Russian readers," which he pro-

Anthony Olcott is assistant professor of Russian at Colgate University.

poses to do by publishing in its entirety Nabokov's novel *The Defense*.[2]
Sergei Zalygin, editor of *Novyi mir*, has promised that his magazine
will publish Nabokov's book on Gogol',[3] and several journals have
published Nabokov poems and other ephemera.

Son of an important White émigré and a prominent life-long critic of
the Soviet regime, Nabokov is only slightly more improbable a figure
for Soviet publication than would be the members of the Acmeist
poetry circle, the only one of whom to become well-known in the USSR
was Anna Akhmatova. For all her circulation after the Khrushchev
thaw, however, several of Akhmatova's works, most notably a poem
about the Terror, *Requiem*, and her poetic autobiography, *Poem without
a Hero*, had never been published in the USSR. At the June 1986
Writers' Congress, poet Andrei Voznesenskii said that the time to
rectify that has come,[4] which has since happened for *Requiem* at least.
He suggested further that the time has also come to publish Evgenii
Zamiatin (author of the first anti-Soviet anti-utopia, *We*), Vladislav
Khodasevich (an important poet of the first emigration), and Fedor
Sologub's *Petty Demon* (a Symbolist depiction of all that is deliberately
ugly and cruel in man), to publish Boris Pasternak in full (by which he
meant publish *Zhivago*), and to publish Nikolai Gumilev.

This last is a particularly striking choice, since Gumilev was a
Tsarist officer and passionate monarchist whom the Bolsheviks shot for
counterrevolutionary activity in 1921, but there is every reason to suppose that Evgenii Evtushenko's prediction, that soon Gumilev will
have a volume in the *Poet's Library* series, will prove correct.[5] Not
only did Evtushenko's article reproduce some few of Gumilev's poems, but other journals have printed his letters to his first wife,
Akhmatova, and others have offered samples of his verse. A third
Acmeist, Osip Mandelstam, who died insane in a gulag transit camp,
has also received unprecedented publicity since Gorbachev's ascension; the journal *Voprosy literatury* has reprinted some of his book
reviews, while the Writers' Union has formed a committee to preserve
Mandelstam's "literary heritage." Given that the committee includes
such powerful literary figures as Daniel Granin, Veniamin Kaverin,
and Lidia Ginzburg[6] (who has written recently about Mandelstam[7]), it
seems possible that Mandelstam will eventually be absorbed more fully
into Russian literature, in part redressing his expulsion under Stalin.

Significantly, this publishing "renaissance" is not restricted only to
what might be called "archeological" finds, artifacts of literary cultures now far removed from the USSR in time and space; an example of

something much closer to the daily reality of the USSR is the publication of a satire on collectivization by Andrei Platonov, *The Sea of Youth*. Although Platonov has satires even more savage (still unpublished in the USSR), this particular work was sufficiently strong that ten years ago, the writer's widow would not even describe the story, let alone permit it to be read. Now it has been printed in *Znamia*.[8]

It might be argued that this literary thaw is no more than old business, an attempt by Russian writers to rectify the fact that, as Academician Dmitri Likhachev put it at the Writers' Congress, "we, in essence, have made a gift to the West of the beginnings of our era,"[9] save that new publications are, if anything, even more startling. Over the past two years it has almost seemed that the editors of journals have begun to vie with one another, to print the most sensational material possible. The greatest part of this outflow of material is muckraking, exposing corruption in trucking (*Neva*, No. 1, 1986), in the museums (*Novyi mir*, No. 2, 1985), factories (*Oktiabr'*, No. 2, 1986), theaters (*Novyi mir*, No. 3, 4, 1986), and kolkhozes (*Nash sovremennik*, No. 1, 1986). Nor has book publishing lagged behind, with exposés of the taxi business (*Taxi Driver* by V. Afonin), procurement (*Pedlars* by A. Kashtanov), and even the militia (*Don't Speed, Pal!* by G. Tsirulis).

A large part of this literature has an even wider target, arguing in essence that it is not simply specific areas of commerce or government which are open to blame, but that something even more fundamental has gone awry. One of the best known of the "village" writers, Valentin Rasputin, in his short novel *Fire*, describes what happens in a Siberian logging town when the warehouses begin to burn. Rasputin shows the entire settlement—which is composed of several former villages relocated into a larger whole because their original sites had been inundated behind a dam—to be degenerate and lawless. The people do not plant, care for livestock, or even raise families.

The hero, Ivan Petrovich, is a militiaman who is able to cope with the flood of hooligans and thugs who work the logging plots only by allowing them freedom to drink, fight, and steal as they wish. When the fire breaks out, taking warehouse after warehouse, it becomes quickly apparent that the town officials have been hoarding large quantities of goods, which the fire of course reduces to garbage. Some of what the fire reveals is food, but a lot of it is consumer goods, in large part imported. What Rasputin is clearly arguing is that the logging enterprise, and by extension the country, is destroying something beautiful, good, and irreplaceable (the forest, the countryside, and the river) in order to purchase the trash of modernity—televisions, motorcycles, and tight jeans.

Even more revealing is the town's reaction. Having assembled to deal collectively with a common threat, the fire brigades quickly degenerate into a drunken Walpurgisnacht of looting. The one entirely positive character in this short angry novel is a crippled half-wit mute who nevertheless knows what the other townsmen do not, that "all the inconvenience and disorder of the world" begin when people "touch what belongs to somebody else."[10] At the novel's end he is beaten to death by marauding drunken thugs. Rasputin permits some light into this story by having Ivan Petrovich visit his son in another, more positive town, but the impact of the book is overwhelmingly negative and dark.

Rasputin himself considers another work "the frankest book we have yet had, written with the blood of [the author's] own heart,"[11] Viktor Astaf'ev's *The Sad Detective*. This novel, the subject of much debate in the Soviet press, berates literature, women, youth, drunkenness, administrators, families, and even the militia, in what amounts to a broadside against current Soviet life. The novel abounds in horror stories, of people starving their children to death out of indifference, of other children abandoned, who must learn to eat cockroaches to survive, of an infant hidden by its mother in the coin locker of a bus station. The hero of the novel is a former militiaman who was wounded while pursuing a motorist who had run down a woman, her baby, and two old pensioners—for which the hero is reprimanded. He lives alone, because his career-minded wife has left him, taking their child. His building is infested with vicious drunkards who attack him, for which he gets in trouble. Curiously, though, Astaf'ev portrays his hero's woes not as injustice, but as the consequence of his having attempted to deal with evil, for police and criminals are facets of the same phenomenon:

> By common sense the earth should long ago have been free of weapons, soldiers, and violence. Their presence is simply dangerous to life, without any sense at all. But instead, monstrous weaponry has reached catastrophic proportions and the number of soldiers in the world is rising, not falling, even though the purpose of those who have put on the military uniform was the same as for all people, to give birth, plough, sow, reap, create. Yet the degenerates keep stealing, killing, and finagling, while against this evil we apply a power which also can't be called good, since the only good power is that which creates, builds. A power that neither

sows nor reaps, but does eat bread, and with butter at that, and that feeds criminals, guarding them so that they won't steal . . . long ago lost the right to call itself a constructive power. . . . There are a lot of [evil people] and they are a well-protected force. For certain of the brighter people lawlessness and law have washed out the dam between themselves, flowing together and dashing in a single wave against the stupefied people, who are waiting lost and doomed for their fates.[12]

Although this novel ends on a faintly hopeful note, with the return of the hero's wife and child, the impact of *The Sad Detective* is pessimistic and ominous, for Astaf'ev plainly states that Soviet society is gravely threatened by indifference to family life:

Dynasties, societies, and empires have turned to dust when the family in them began to disintegrate, if he and she get lost, without finding one another. Dynasties, societies, and empires that do not create families or that destroy family stability begin to boast of their progress and rattle their weapons; in dynasties, empires, and societies where the family fell to pieces, so too did commonality; evil began to overwhelm good, and the earth began to gape beneath their feet, to swallow up the riff-raff who, without any justification for doing so, called themselves people.[13]

As strong as this warning may sound, it has been outdone, by no less a figure than Chinghiz Aitmatov, member of the directorate of the Writers' Union, and one of the most visible writers in the USSR, whose new novel, *The Execution Block*, must surely be the most striking work to date in the Gorbachev "thaw." Part of the reason for this is journalistic, for the novel concerns a youth gang that gathers wild hemp in Kazakhstan, to sell as narcotics. Since the appearance of *The Execution Block*, Soviet authorities have begun to speak of a drug abuse problem of massive scale, too large to be ignored any longer. Newspapers have begun to write of the need to cure addicts, to halt the illegal cultivation of hemp and poppies, and to tighten controls on prescription medicines—all issues that were introduced by Aitmatov's novel.

What is even more startling, in the larger context of Soviet history, is the explanation Aitmatov gives for this drug culture, for he argues openly that these drug-runners are products of a breakdown of culture in Soviet life, and that the only remedy for them is religion. Given that Aitmatov is of Muslim background (a religious tradition of which he wrote very positively in his previous novel, *The Day Lasts More Than One Hundred Years*, it seems doubly odd that he chose as his hero one Avdii Kallistratov, a Russian, an expelled seminarian, and a Christian.

As Aitmatov explained it in an interview, he chose this hero precisely because of the need to introduce a Christ figure, someone who would take upon himself the suffering of the world.[14] This Kallistratov does. He attempts to turn the degenerate gang of drug-runners to worship of "contemporary-God," for which they chuck him from a speeding freight train. He next attempts to save a similarly drink-addled group who have been machine-gunning wild antelope herds, and the irate men quite literally crucify him. As if to make the point even more unmistakable, Aitmatov also includes Christ as a character, in a scene portraying the last interview with Pilate. Moreover, throughout the novel Aitmatov capitalizes the word *Bog* (God), which has not been the Soviet practice for almost seventy years, and which prompted one hostile critic of the book to remark, "it is more than strange to read such a thing in the Soviet press."[15]

In sum, the impression conveyed by recent Soviet publications is that the Gorbachev years have ushered in a period of unprecedented freedom, as writers may now discuss virtually anything, from religion to sex, from drugs to ecology, in violation of nearly every canon of Soviet literature. Perhaps the best measure of the departure from past practice comes from those who oppose it, such as the conservative Boris Kunitsyn, who writes urgently that sex has invaded Russian literature (Artsybashev was nothing compared to what is happening now, he fulminates), that recent books depict the overwhelming materialism of youth, and that all signs point to what Kunitsyn calls "creeping empiricism":

> So this "creeping empiricism" which has gotten around the locks and bolts (which certain authors and readers understand sometimes as a form of the highest daring) in my view has a quality which is far from harmless: it fosters the illusion that all is permitted! All is possible![16]

There is some reason to share Kunitsyn's conclusion, if not his alarm. Evtushenko, for example, has spoken openly of the need to write honestly about collectivization,[17] and editors have made broad hints about future works on such sore points of Soviet history as Lysenkoism[18] and Afghanistan.[19]

It is therefore tempting to conclude, on the basis of this and other evidence, that the Gorbachev era will be one of cultural achievement and latitude; to do so, however, requires two assumptions, neither of which may be justified.

Problems of interpretation

The first assumption is that publication automatically implies a readership, that the new freedom to create is accompanied by new freedom to think. There are very real grounds for supposing that there is actually little connection between writer and reader, or at least a good deal less than in the days when, to paraphrase Mandelstam, Russia took poetry seriously enough to shoot poets. Poets and other writers are no longer shot, and there is evidence to suggest that the importance of the word has fallen accordingly. Statistical verification of the point is of course impossible, partly because of the peculiarities of the Soviet book trade, partly because of the lack of statistics, and partly because even such figures as are available are suspect, due to the distorting effect of the image of self which respondents wish to present to their interviewers. Andrei Voznesenskii may still be justified in his claim that "Russia is the last reading nation on earth,"[20] but a patchwork of available figures and subjective impression gives reason to think that Nikolai Miroshnichenko may also have some justification for his bitter observation that Russia should instead now be called the "most *dancing* nation" on earth.[21] People in the USSR seem to be reading less, and reading less seriously when they do. A sociological treatise from Kirghizia, for example, using a sample base of unstated size and composition, says that among men surveyed, only 38.3 percent read journals "regularly," while 20.3 percent read them "rarely"; 45 percent of men surveyed read books regularly (including nonfiction and technical books having to do with their work), while 14.4 percent read rarely. Even more striking is the survey finding that reading drops with age, so that only 33 percent of respondents age 51–60 read regularly, while 23.9 percent read rarely. In sum, 51.4 percent of all respondents said they read a newspaper every day, 35.4 percent read journals daily, 44.3 percent read books daily (again, without distinction as to type of book), and 71.9 percent watch television.[22]

The nature of Soviet reading habits might also be questioned in view of a letter to *Literaturnaia gazeta* from the chairman of the Department of Applied Sociology at Latvian University, who pointed out that while *possession* of books may be a cultural plus, possession does not mean use. He cites a study by his department of people who had purchased a complete collected works of "the classic Latvian author Jaunsudrabin," which showed that only 23 percent of these people had ever so much as *opened* the first volume, let alone read it.[23]

More subjective sources also seem to suggest that the Soviet passion
for reading is being supplanted by other activities. Many critics complain that young people don't read at all,[24] and the papers have been
filled with articles by critics and writers alarmed that the recent cur-
riculum changes in the schools are coming at the expense of literature.[25] At least one fictional portrait of a Soviet middle-class woman
shows that she is forced by the demands of a busy Soviet bourgeois life
to give up reading even for show, "to keep up with the latest."[26]

What is being read is also changing, it seems. Critics complain of
indifferent or lazy readers, observing, in the words of one, that "today
what is read mostly is not the classics, not the authors of our brilliant
military prose, but slight detective novels, ours and imports, and science fiction, most of it far from scientific."[27] The same complaint is
made more aphoristically by the critic Natalia Ivanova, who observes
that " 'Milord Stupid' is bought up rapidly, while Grant Matevosian lies
on the shelves"[28] (Milord Stupid is a shorthand reference from the
Nekrasov poem *Who Is Happy in Russia?* for the philistine reading
tastes of tsarist landowners; Matevosian is a talented Armenian writer
of village prose).

Nor is this crumbling of culture restricted to readers. Another critic
has complained that:

> very often the contemporary writer is, unfortunately, simply of little
> culture. Nor is this simply a matter of upbringing and education, though
> this is its foundation. The genealogy of contemporary literature on the
> whole is not of good blood, and even, I would say, has a great deal of
> "bastard blood," without cultural tradition. . . . This is the source for
> the obvious preference for quantity over quality, the abundance of profes-
> sionals at the same time that artistry is disappearing, with functionalism,
> "concern," and fussing reigning in place of organic and free artistic
> expression. Has not the dominant stimulus of the literary process become
> the drive to hang on, set up, break in, be seen, be noticed, to flourish and
> to thrive?[29]

In the same vein the editor of the youth journal *Iunost'* complains of
"Young authors spoiled by seminars, festivals, the press, and fore-
words by the venerable, [who] often behave simply aggressively when
we ask that they be more demanding of themselves and return their
manuscripts to them."[30]

One young writer, Tat'iana Tolstaia, has termed this phenomenon
"pseudoculture," which begins, she says, in the schools. She cites

examples from the standard literary texts, such as a famous poem by Fet, which for a decade has been printed without its last quatrain, while other poems are misquoted in ways that utterly destroy rhythm and rhyme. Equally the texts abound in the ignorant and false; she cites one poet's gushings about the warmth he has for words sharing the root *rod* (meaning birth, generation), one of which is *smorodina* (black currant). In fact, Tolstaia observes dryly, that word comes from the verb *smerdet'* (to stink).[31]

Such printed comments bear out more subjective impressions that the reading habits of the Soviet citizenry have moved from serious to light, just as the recreational function of literature has risen at the expense of the didactic, causing Academician Likhachev to fret that "Art must strive to raise each of us to the level of its highest accomplishment, its peaks, and not try to be understood by the minds of the lazy and incurious."[32] Obviously, such a warning would not be necessary, were not the tendency in the opposite direction. The most popular author in the USSR is probably Valentin Pikul', who writes slightly salacious quasihistorical novels; the most popular poet is without question Vladimir Vysotskii, who in fact was a balladeer, an enormously talented songwriter, but no poet. The most popular books are detective novels, science fiction, and thrillers, while horror and sex have begun to emerge as genres; *Zvezda* devoted three issues to a translation of Stephen King's *Firestarter*, while several novels have raised critics' eyebrows with their sexual frankness.[33]

The second assumption underlying a conclusion that the USSR is enjoying a cultural renaissance under Gorbachev is that literature is representative of culture in general, which is difficult to substantiate at a distance, because other cultural artifacts—films, dance, theater, television, art—are much less accessible outside the USSR. Equally important is that the relative availability of such things is very different inside the USSR and out. Television, and some films, will reach audiences far larger than those ever achieved by, for example, Aitmatov's new novel, while other films, some plays, and some art will circulate widely in élite circles and in the West, without ever reaching an average Soviet audience. A researcher is therefore always in danger of basing conclusions about the broader cultural life upon intellectual products of which most Soviet citizens are unaware, while himself remaining ignorant of the true stuff of the average Soviet citizen's "cultural life."

Still, for all the inaccessibility of the products themselves, available literature suggests that many of the same ills that beset literature also infest other cultural spheres. The word of the moment is *seriatina*, greyness, which critics find everywhere. For example, one says that films have become so predictably formulaic and dull that people simply stay away,[34] which means, as another points out, that the film studios are wasting a lot of the government's money.[35] An account of a film festival in Alma-Ata complains that "it was harder to leave [the festival] without a prize than with one."[36] An interesting feature of the festival was that the directors of the films that the readers of *Sovetskii ekran* had voted *least* interesting were supposed to be present to explain their failures; for unspecified but probably not very surprising reasons, they did not appear.

The theater has played an important part in the Gorbachev "thaw," for it was productions of such plays as *The Suit* and *Silver Anniversary*—which examined the corrupt administrative behavior that Gorbachev was to make his target—that first signaled that some sort of change was in the wind. Nor is the change in theater simply one of topic, making the theater an arm of journalism; there have also been important innovations in staging and presentation, reaching even such untouchable classics as *Three Sisters*, which Iurii Liubimov redid in the handsome new Taganka. Again, the best indicator of change in the theater may come from someone hostile to it, such as V. Mishin, former head of the Komsomol, who complained that all the new plays had as their heroes "some cynical youth of advanced years who strolls weightily about, a foppish dependent wearing the famous jeans, someone both infantile and programmatic."[37]

In the same vein critics complain of the dullness even of the circuses and museums, which for all their abundance are boring and identical; as one critic wrote of museums, "the absence of a spiritual, emotional atmosphere seems almost to be the law for modern museums."[38] Other spheres of art are even more difficult to discuss, given their unexportability; still, newspaper accounts of, for example, the open-air art market at Bitsa Park in Moscow suggest that there is considerable ferment in these cultural areas as well. But again, as in the case of literature, there is reason to be cautious in concluding that agitation for less greyness and greater adventurousness means necessarily greater intellectual freedom for the mass of Soviet citizens.

That a theater in Moscow is freer to experiment does not necessarily tell us much about the state of the theater in general. For all the attention a given play at the Taganka or any other fashionable theater may attract, its potential audience is extremely limited; the unobtainability of tickets is one of the clichés of Soviet life. Much more typical of Soviet theaters are those lampooned by L. Korsunskii in a (fictitious) conversation between a bored theater-goer, who wants his money back, and the theater director, who protests that he is required to put on four plays a year—one industrial, one international, one about Lenin, and, "highly desirable," a classic. The hostile patron replies:

> *Viewer:* So put on good plays.
> *Administrator:* Just plain good ones? And who's going to put on the necessary plays then?
> *Viewer:* The only necessary play is a very good one.
> *Administrator:* That's almost anti-ideological (*bezideishchina*)![39]

Nor is it possible to be certain about the degree to which availability of some cultural product implies its use or acceptance, as the situation in two other culture spheres suggests. Almost no mention seems to have been made of the world of dance, perhaps because the audience for classical dance is relatively small and stable, while innovation of another sort has brought dance, of a kind, to the masses, in the form of leggy night-club hoofers in quite striking degrees of undress. Related to this is the situation in music, where the high cultural world of serious music has remained apparently unchanged, while the lower one of popular music has been under steady and enormous pressure from rock-and-roll. Despite the official Ministry of Culture position that "Rock is an alien phenomenon for us, and we have no wish to encourage it,"[40] pop-rock-disco blares from virtually every café, restaurant, and club, and is even carried on the radio and heard in most stores and even the airplanes of the USSR. "Classics" such as Rolling Stones or Beatles songs have become standards of the repertoires, leaving as the only area of contention the newer fads of heavy metal and punk—the Party seems to fare as poorly in its efforts to discourage these as any American parent of teenagers. "We listen to heavy metal and don't plan to stop!" an anonymous teen boasts in an article in *Sobesednik*.[41]

The general standard of popularity is probably the singer Alla Pugacheva, who, one conservative critic observes testily, was first on the list when a teacher asked her class to list their heroes; in second and third place were the hockey goalie Tretiak and the cosmonauts.[42] And what, the same critic asks, creates this "poverty of culture"?

> Here comes a singer out on the stage. Her success comes not from the beauty of her voice, not from the nobility of her manner (which is clearly

taken from the tarty beauties of the cabaret), not from her attempt to touch the soul with the uplifting power of art. Her strange wrenching yelps sound hysterical somehow, brawling, petty. . . . She speaks openly of her hatred for the opinions others form of her, she is defiant about her retinue of lovers, and she sings about a tawdry game of love. And the hall explodes in admiration.[43]

It will be noted that this critic, like Mishin, is complaining not so much about the message as about the manner in which it is conveyed, the appearance of the performers, their carriage and dress. This too is a part of culture, given the extraordinarily wide fields of meaning in Russian of *kul'tura* and the related terms, *kul'turnost'* and *nekul'-turnost'*; particularly these last two can cover anything from knowledge of ancient languages to not spitting in public places. Part of the reason this field of meaning is so broad is that it is based upon the unarticulated assumption that culture is an unbroken continuum of approved and disapproved behavior, each segment of which implies the other. Thus the man who spits in public or otherwise behaves boorishly could not possibly speak correctly, treat his family correctly, or hold a respectable job, while the man who does not spit in public will be assumed to be capable of all the rest, particularly if he dresses well and carries a briefcase. It is this assumption that has given such decorousness to Soviet public life; to a far greater extent than has ever been the case in America or other western societies, the USSR once enjoyed a broad consensus about the nature of "proper" behavior, and the result was the much-remarked cleanliness and order of Soviet cities.

As some of the quotations above suggest, there is reason to suppose this consensus is unravelling. Iurii Nagibin in his novella *Voyage to the Islands* recounts a trip to the Solovetskii Islands, an important historical and cultural site for Russians. Save for the main character and his friend, the tourists are uniformly ignorant, petty, disrespectful, uncultured oafs, reaching their nadir in one beer-bellied, redheaded fool. When this clown climbs into an ancient sarcophagus to show off, the hero, able to bear it no longer, shoves him to the ground. Furious, the fellow strikes back, shrieking "You're a son of a bitch, you're going to pay for everything! The whole stink's because of the likes of you! My whole life you and your type have been in my way!"[44]

In large part Rasputin's *The Fire* and Astaf'ev's *Sad Detective* are portraits of this same boorishness, what the British call yobbo culture. Astaf'ev in particular dwells on characters like the drunken hag who loiters in the marketplace, or the drunken thugs who gather in the stairwell of his building. Even fiction that has nothing to do with the concerns of Rasputin and Astaf'ev reflects this yobboism, which suggests that it is quite widespread. A story set in Leningrad, for example, contains this incidental moment:

> . . . three lads about twenty. They were making such a racket that there might have been at least ten of them. On the right, striding along, was a mug with wide-flung bowlegs and the shoulders of a wrestler. He was tugging at the guitar strings as hard as he could, wrenching out a totally paralyzing din, which he accompanied with tawdry, dishevelled yelps. Next to him was a pleasant enough man in a T-shirt which said in English "Guns don't die—people do." His head was shaved bald and he had a small dark mustache. His expression was aggressive . . . and so naturally a bit criminal. The third was a tall fellow, limp somehow, narrow in the shoulders and barely able to stand. He kept bending from side to side, like a boiled macaroni. His eyes were so empty that they seemed like open blanks. The tall one's mouth was wide open and emitting some sort of senseless ugly howl. . . .
>
> "Hey pops! Wipe your blower and clamp your cake hole, you stink of garlic, you son of a bitch!" [one of them said to Mark].
>
> The criminal slowly took his fist from his pocket and suddenly, easily, hit Mark on the chin with the back of his hand.
>
> Mark flew up, then slammed down onto the sidewalk.[45]

Certainly part of this fraying of civic culture is a result of an explosion of substance abuse, both the familiar alcohol problem and the newer one of drugs. As is generally the case in the USSR, there are no firm statistics, but the level of drug use seems high; certainly there is no shortage of material for abuse. An article on the drug problem in Dnepropetrovsk says that there are eight thousand hectares *legally* planted to hemp in the area, and that hemp planting in the USSR has increased 25-fold in the past 25 years; Dnepropetrovsk also enjoys its local proportion of the poppies necessary to produce the five to six thousand tons of poppy *seeds* that the Ukraine requires every year for its baking needs.[46] Even more threatening, from a Soviet point of view, is the implication of the letter in *Literaturnaia gazeta* that first brought the drug issue to the surface; there a mother from Odessa describes her two sons, both addicts, implying that one of them had been a model of behavior until he joined the Army, where he had acquired his addiction. Not only would this tend to confirm rumors of drug abuse among Soviet soldiers, but even to widen it, for the son had served not in Afghanistan, but on Sakhalin.

Disturbing as an explosion of drug abuse would be, the available literature seems to regard it primarily as a symptom of wider processes of disaffection, especially among the young. As mentioned above, Astaf'ev has written bitterly of the breakdown of the family, while Aitmatov, in an interview, held it responsible for the problems of Soviet youth:

> I wouldn't want to be young now. I feel uncomfortable somehow among the youth of today. Probably we are guilty ourselves for what is happening with the unfledged, young part of society. In conditions of plenty—and say what you will, we have plenty; we have no hungry, poor, or homeless—the cost of spiritual education, the absence of a high internal culture, are leading to consumerism, nest-feathering, "thing-ism," when the material factor goes to the head of the line and the spiritual potential drops to zero. I think that in significant degree the cause here is the family, and even more the school.[47]

The same points are raised by the editor of *Oktiabr'* in a meditation on the reasoning behind the programs mandated at the Twenty-seventh Party Congress:

> We have turned the engineer into a disinterested laborer who earns so little that he runs off to sell apples or beer because he can make money doing so. We take no account of the fact that man is born to strengthen himself on earth . . . with goods, with work. I would say that the first cell where this strengthening takes place is the family. But how can an engineer strengthen himself when he earns so little that he can't feel himself master in the family and so is disgruntled with life? In the past a peasant, the simplest, most ordinary peasant, knew that the well-being of his family depended upon his industriousness, and so he would get up earlier, go out to the fields earlier, and in this way gain stature in the eyes of his family, in the eyes of the people around him. The family, as is well known, is the first cell of the state, and the well-being of the family is the well-being of the country.
>
> But nowadays the work of a kolkhoznik or laborer is so regulated that he can't earn any more than is allowed, and he enters a family which he can't fully guarantee to support, which makes him feel helpless. So he flings himself into all manner of letting off steam, including drunkenness. He begins to raise hell, and watching all of this are the children . . . the daughter follows the mother, the son the father. For some reason we have forgotten this entirely and think that only the day-care centers and kindergartens can take care of everything. They can't replace a strong, fundamental family.[48]

In a society in which half of all marriages now end in divorce, parents easily abandon children, and the old are abandoned to state care, the "strong, fundamental" family of which Anan'ev speaks would seem to be almost a statistical rarity.

Understanding *glasnost'*

As bleak as this picture of the cultural fabric of Soviet life may seem, two important cautions should be kept in mind. First is that publicity should not be confused with reality, and the significance and effect of this apparent cultural disintegration exaggerated. For all the sensational qualities of recent disclosures in the Soviet press, the horrors revealed are still less than what one might find in a single issue of the *New York Daily News*; in fact, it may well be that the distance between the picture one might form there, of a corrupt, disintegrating, and violent America, and what most Americans feel to be the truth about our country, is about the same as the distance between press accounts and reality in the USSR.

The second point is that, while this sudden eruption of criticism may be partly a product of changes in the Soviet cultural fabric, it is certainly a product of changes in the official attitude toward information; the regime has chosen to use *glasnost'*, or openness about societal ills, as a means of social control. Seen in this light, much of the recent burst of criticism is simply pent-up carping, airing publicly what people have said privately for years, because (in the words of one critic):

> There are conflicts in Soviet history that must be "overcome" in literature, so that the past can be left behind forever. . . . the main thing . . . is that [truth-speakers] will inspire new forces of truth and optimism in our literature, for a tragedy overcome publicly, and admitted for what it was, already ceases to be a source of doubt and suffering.[49]

As the extraordinary amount of critical material makes plain, however, there is some question about the effect this new openness will have. It is hard not to wonder, for example, whether the *glasnost'* campaign might not ultimately bring grief to those who bear the bad news. A Soviet populace which for years has been told it has full employment, few social problems, good harvests, and the approval of history is now suddenly confronted with widespread accounts of drug abuse, AIDS, bribery, kidnappings, infanticide, riots, atomic disasters, ship wrecks, and even natural disasters (which because they weren't reported didn't exist under previous rulers); people might reasonably conclude in such circumstances that the problem lies not with them, but with the man in charge, who should be keeping an eye on such things.

Certainly there is no clear evidence that *glasnost'* has had any positive impact on the way society works. As many writers pointed out from the Writers' Congress podium, everyone complains of dull writing, but no one dares name a dull writer, let alone prevent him from publishing. Some speakers also observed that many of the same writers who now denounce corruption were lauding it a few years before.[50] Nor is this imbalance between what is said and what is done restricted to literature. The press is full of accounts of official promises made but never kept, as in the reconstruction of Kizhi, which has effectively destroyed the ancient churches[51]; or the thoughtless way streets are renamed, destroying old neighborhoods[52]; or projects such as the construction of the Borovitskii Metro station in Moscow, which threatens to take the Rumiantsev building of Lenin Library into the pit with it.[53] Valentin Rasputin told the Writers' Union that a much bally-hooed committee to save Lake Baikal never met,[54] and the government has been exposed baldly in its simultaneous attempts to appease Russians who want the northern rivers diversion project stopped, and Central Asians who need the water the project would provide. Even though abandoning of the river diversion project was bruited in a front-page communiqué from the Central Committee, a later announcement said the halt was temporary and might be reconsidered.[55]

There is evidence that the Soviet public has remained skeptical and apprehensive about *glasnost'*, a caution understandable in a place where policy shifts can be both swift and dangerous. This skepticism is probably not always as bald as that shown in a note passed to Boris El'tsin at a meeting with Moscow workers, which reportedly said: "Khrushchev tried to make us all dress like peasants, but he didn't succeed and neither will you. We've always stolen and we'll keep on stealing."[56] A more common form of disassociation, though not always as open, is probably that exercised by the writer Anatolii Lanshchikov, who sent as his answer to a *Literaturnaia gazeta* poll about the Eighth Writers' Congress the exact same answer that he had sent five years earlier, after the Seventh.[57] Another curious confirmation of this same distancing comes from a new column appearing in *Literaturnaia gazeta*, "7×7,"in which seven writers are asked to name the television programs they had most enjoyed over the week, and the ones they had found dull, a waste of time. Introduced in mid-summer 1986, the column at first listed both good and bad shows; but, increasingly, respondents now either skip the second question entirely, or, if they do answer it, complain in general terms, without naming specific programs. Perhaps it should come as no surprise that schoolchildren who were asked why heroes of socialist labor perform their extraordinary feats reportedly gave three possible explanations: the Stakhanovites wanted more money, were seeking the praise of their superiors, or wanted to get their names in the newspaper.[58]

Indeed, there is rather an air about the *glasnost'* campaign of many voices shrieking into deaf ears. As mentioned above, reading seems to be down, as is movie attendance, and there is a clear swing from art as education to art as entertainment, with the general result that the power of the word, of the artist, seems to have shrunk. As Andrei Sakharov noted wryly upon his release from internal exile, the government now says things for which it once sent people to prison. Where Aleksandr Solzhenitsyn might once have seemed a serious opponent to an established government, based solely on his writings, writers seem able now to say virtually anything they wish, with little apparent effect. As one critic observed, in trying to explain the current popularity of theaters of mime in the USSR, it is almost as though people have tired of *words*.[59]

If it is possible to judge the distribution of social habits by the stridency and frequency of attacks upon them, then the USSR would seem to be entering a period, not of cultural renaissance, but of indifference to civic life, a time of private concerns. The youth papers portray adolescents interested only in rock music, clothes, and pleasures of the flesh, while adults seem just as self-involved. If this is true, then it seems logical that the cultural world will have to back away from *glasnost'*, once it becomes clear that admission of past shortcomings does nothing to prevent future ones. Recent comments by Writers' Union secretaries Karpov and Kuznetsov suggest that the limits of *glasnost'* may already have been reached, and—given the similarity of their statements—that those limits have been set as stated policy. In Kuznetsov's words:

As a result of a whole complex of reasons, over the last few years there have been alarming aberrations, when, for example, that line of patriotic culture represented by names like M. Gorky, A. Tolstoi, A. Fadeev, D. Furmanov, N. Ostrovskii, A. Malyshkin, M. Sholokhov, and A. Tvardovskii suddenly was pushed into the shade, while center stage was taken by another line . . . represented by B. Pasternak, A. Akhmatova, M. Tsvetaeva, O. Mandelstam, M. Bulgakov, and others. . . . we are obligated to overcome these historical aberrations by force of knowledge, culture, education, and an understanding of the social realities of things.[60]

And Karpov was, if anything, even less ambiguous, saying that:

Certain people have emerged (and not just among writers) who perceive democracy as total license . . . and take on the role of exposer, their genre being letters "to the top" and their sources of information being . . . keyholes, rumors, and scandal.
. . . unfortunately these drones in our literary environment . . . distract and divert attention from the main work and problems, and consume much time, strength, and . . . nervous energy.[61]

And that "main work"? A writer at another conference put it bluntly: "The task of literature today is to help the Party limit the retardation of human consciousness in recognizing the historical act which has already occurred and in which we are not only witnesses, but also participants."[62]

The obvious difficulty is that to retract *glasnost'* would do little more than return the USSR to the time when, in Evgenii Sidorov's words, "vulgar optimism . . . covered everything with a vigorous phrase and a glistening smile,"[63] while productivity collapsed, the family disintegrated, and corruption flourished. It is probably this perception of cynicism and falsehood which accounts for the intense interest now shown in religion and the spiritual bases of society. Valentin Kataev writes in his novella *Dry Inlet* of two sons of a priestly family, whose upbringing gave them qualities that made them valuable Soviet citizens—a distinguished Army officer and an important scientist.[64] Astaf'ev has written of the moral values of Orthodoxy, as has Vasilii Bykov, while Aitmatov and Fazil Iskander have both written of the enduring values of their Islamic heritage.

Although this renewed interest in religion is unquestionably bound up with issues of nationalism, especially in the case of Orthodoxy, a great deal of it also stems from a widespread realization that the Soviet Union remains impaled on the paradox of having established a materialist system in which people are expected to participate for spiritual reasons. Having successfully inculcated in the bulk of its population the conviction that there is no afterlife, no higher reckoning, the USSR must now cope with people determined to have as many of life's material advantages as they can grab without being caught. There seems a growing awareness among the intellectuals that such a system is unworkable; as Evgenii Evtushenko put it in a letter to *Komsomol'skaia pravda*:

> The problem is the inundation of the country by nonprofessionals. For all the kindness of his personal character, an unprofessional doctor is a potential killer. Yet in some sense every nonprofessional is a killer. The unprofessional writer is a killer of guiltless paper, the unprofessional economist is a killer of the people's money. The unprofessional builder is a killer of building materials, the unprofessional reshaper of nature is a killer of lakes and rivers, the unprofessional newsman is a killer of your time and mine.[65]

Academic Likhachev's call for a kind of moral regeneration is even more straighforward:

> I am certain the greatest economic success will come from moral successes, from developing the culture of memory, from societal assistance to the old and the sick, from the resurrection in society of moral categories like honor. . . . The concept of honor has, entirely without justification, disappeared from our life.[66]

This regeneration is being widely discussed under the rubric of "culture" (in Evtushenko's words, "the source of morality is culture"[67]), but is clearly being understood as at least partly religious by the authorities, who reject it unconditionally. As Suren Kaltakhchian, an important Party ideologue, warns:

> Finally, we cannot ignore that our literature and art, which have made invaluable contributions to the atheist education of the workers, have in recent years let weaken their attention to the problems of atheism. And what is even worse, in some literary works, movies, and paintings there is plainly admiration for church ritual, lipsmacking over the "charms" of the Lives of the Saints, the Elders, church life, and religious morality. Our younger generation has the right to hope that cultural figures will make a worthy contribution to the completion of atheist education, in the development and dissemination of new Soviet rituals and habits, in the strengthening of communist morality, to which the hyprocrisy and sanctimony of religious morality are alien.[68]

The picture that emerges seems familiar. *Glasnost'* appears increasingly to have limits, and it is ever clearer that openness—in journalism, in literature, in culture in general—is viewed not as an absolute good, but rather as a tool, useful only as long as it produces the results desired by the Party and its planners. Moreover, this tool would seem a self-limiting one, if the Party continues to insist on following old principles no matter how flagrantly they contradict new truths, a likelihood which Aitmatov sketches succinctly in *The Execution Block*. One of his heroes, a highly productive, responsible shepherd, has argued that productivity would be raised if the herders could work as though they were private units, responsible for gathering their own fodder, protecting their own sheep, and so reaping profits based on their own effectiveness; he is answered acidly by the kolkhoz's party organizer (of whom the herder observes, "I feed and nourish you, not the other way about"[69]):

> "How long are you going to confuse the people with your dubious proposals? The form of production relationships within the socialist collective was long ago defined by history. But you want the herder to be like an owner, to decide who to work with, who not to, and how much to pay to whom. What is this? Nothing less than an attack on history, on our revolutionary achievements, an attempt to place economics before politics. You are arguing solely from the narrow interests of your band of sheep. For you this is the question of all questions. But beyond the sheep band is the raion, the oblast, the country! What do you want to bring us to, the rejection of socialist principles of management?"[70]

At the same time, it should be noted that the USSR has not only changed sufficiently to permit publication of this fairly open satire of party obtuseness, but even has apparently accepted the wisdom of the herder's argument; one of the activities to be permitted under the new laws on limited private enterprise is sheepherding.

The "why" of *glasnost'*

Still, for all the changes, it seems probable that the Soviet Union will remain in a state of tension, trying to use culture, literature, the arts, and the media as means to motivate and reward its populace, while trying to contain the course these activities take. Because this exercise seems inherently contradictory, it is likely that the tension will grow, particularly given the stresses now manifest in Soviet culture. Three oppositions in particular seem worth citing, because of the important roles they are likely to play in the further development of the USSR.

One of these is youth vs. age. For all the discussion of the Gorbachev "revolution" sweeping out the old guard, the ranks of the cultural establishments seem secure. Several writers at the Writers' Congress complained of the established writers' dominance even of the regional and youth presses, which were intended as vehicles for new writers. A writer could be considered "young" well into his or her fifth decade, as the make-up of the delegates to the congress demonstrates; a full 15 percent were over seventy, while 60 percent were in their fifties and sixties. A spare 3 percent of the writers present were under 40, while only three people, or .5 percent of the delegates, were under 35 (two of them from one republic).[71] Soviet authorities perceive a danger in this underrepresentation, no doubt because they are aware of the important generational differences between those who recall the war, the Terror, and the other dark periods of Soviet life, and those who have grown up in the well-fed, corrupt, and plentiful years of the Brezhnev era. In fact, given the harsh worlds of their parents and grandparents, the current group of young people may be the first Soviet citizens who can be said to *have* a youth, making the whole phenomenon of adolescence something with which the authorities have no experience. These young people, and particularly the Russian youth, are a relatively small, pampered group (how many, for instance, are only children?), upon which a great part of the Soviet future must rest. While culture is obviously going to have to find some way to involve and motivate this group, the impression conveyed by most sources is that youth remains a total mystery, for the authorities, for their parents, and probably for themselves. In most accounts, the better of the young people seem careerist and technical, while the worse seem pleasure-centered to the point of degeneracy; neither group seems socially concerned. It is true that youth invariably seems worse to its elders than it in fact proves to be, but there is nonetheless real cause for concern.

It seems reasonable to expect that among the tools used to reach youth will be culture. What exactly those blandishments might be touches upon a second tension, that of art as enlightenment vs. art as entertainment, which might more easily be described as high culture and low. A large part of what we in the West see as cultural ferment touches only a small and select group of intellectuals. For all the passion over whether or not to publish Gumilev, Pasternak, or Nabokov, the potential audience for such writers can not number more than a few multiples of a thousand. It is true that the influence of this small group is far greater than its numbers, and that it may have as much impact upon Soviet culture that the intelligentsia can read Nabokov, as a *symbol* of cultural latitude, as it would if everyone were reading him. There is a paradox here, though, because it is generally assumed that such forbidden fruits are *already* enjoyed by the intelligentsia—indeed that access to Nabokov, Gumilev, and the others is one of the definitions of being an intellectual. The regime's move to legalize what already exists can thus be seen to be a sign of weakness rather than strength, reinforcing the message that "if we keep on doing as we please, eventually they'll have to make it legal."

This interpretation makes the situation in the more popular, accessible media of film and television complex and somewhat contradictory. While it seems unlikely that ideological reins will be loosened here, and indeed that the ideological content will grow, the authorities will also have to reckon with audiences who, if they aren't interested, will simply not attend or watch. Like it or not, the popular media will probably have to take account of popular taste, since an audience must be grabbed before it can be lectured; so it seems reasonable to expect racier themes, more sexually oriented material, more rock-like music, and, despite the recent law against violent video cassettes, more violence. Moreover, if this audience has learned that its indifference can bring change in the media—and it seems that it has—then the pressure will always be to subordinate didacticism to entertainment, in the interest of reaching an audience. Since the variety and number of amusements has grown in the USSR, as in the West, the consumers of culture have choices, and the media must seek audiences, rather than the other way about.

The third tension, which may well prove the most important of all in the future USSR, is that of Russian vs. non-Russian. As used in this paper, the term "Soviet culture" is essentially Russo-centric, or Russian-defined, as in fact it is in the USSR. Most of the media, most of the artists, and most of the assumptions underlying the definition of "culture" are Russian, because historically Russians both dominated and defined the arts. Even today in the Soviet context, languages other than Russian are by definition parochial, because any writer (or filmmaker or playwright or songwriter) who wishes to reach an all-union audience must do so in Russian. In the past, and to some extent today, non-Russian writers did this through translation, but increasing numbers of them, schooled in Soviet schools, reared on Soviet television, and entertaining Soviet ambitions, are composing directly in Russian.

It is here that the tension is felt most acutely in the arts, for it has not been resolved what Russian is to be—the expression and product of Russian culture, so leaving Russians forever the arbiters of grammar, pronunciation, and usage, or the medium of communication among Soviet citizens, upon which all members of the USSR have equally valid claim. Both definitions have proponents, and the pressures they apply can be expected to grow. By now, whole generations of Russians and non-Russians alike have grown up watching the same movies, reading the same books, studying the same school curricula, and sharing the same experiences. It seems reasonable, then, that a non-Russian Soviet youth of today who aspires to rise above a local, parochial level will have the same expectations for the future as will his Russian counterpart, meaning in culture that he will feel as competent to address Soviet issues as will any Russian.

One area in which this may have interesting repercussions is in the broader understanding of ''culture,'' since available evidence suggests that the breakdown of public order and morality which so upsets Astaf'ev, Nagibin, and Rasputin is much more widespread among Slavs, and particularly Russians, than it is in areas where traditional cultures continue to have a stronger hold, as in the Caucasus and Central Asia. Certainly these areas seem to be spared many of the alcohol, divorce, and child-abuse problems of the Russian areas, which would suggest that the temptation for non-Russians to preach to Russians, or at least to reject Russians' preaching to them, might be strong.

For their part, many Russians without question feel culturally embattled, surrounded by barbarians. Witness the complaint about Aitmatov, that ''sometimes he tries to show off with rare, unaccustomed word combinations and occasionally he uses words imprecisely or inappropriately . . . [because] for Aitmatov Russian is after all a second language.''[72] This seems a churlish way to characterize a man who has been speaking Russian for at least forty years, and writing in it for twenty (and what complaint would this critic make about Nabokov's English?). Similarly, with reference to *The Execution Block*, the complaint has been made that Aitmatov shows ''incompetence . . . in questions about the life of the contemporary Orthodox church.''[73] No similar charge has been leveled at, for example, Andrei Platonov, for his depictions of Central Asia in the novellas ''Dzhan'' and ''Takyr.''

The implication of such attitudes is that Russian culture and, by extension, Russians, have an innate superiority which permits them to deal with all of Soviet life, while non-Russians, particularly the Caucasians, Central Asians, and native Siberians, are relegated to local color. It is presumably to this that the Daghestani Ramzul Gamzatov referred in his Writers' Congress address when he said, "It's a bad thing, when business-trip rhymes or tourist poems, this dagger-and-bracelet literature, is taken as deeply national. Often these kind of works appear in Russian before they do in their native language."[74]

The fervor with which Russians have been defending the sanctity of the Russian language and Russian culture suggests that the counterpressure by non-Russians is very strong; certain writers at least sound almost apocalyptic as they describe the problem. Kunitsyn, for example, writes:

> We have carried and preserved in purity the great Russian language through all of our historical catastrophes, passed down to us by our grandfathers and fathers. . . . You can be sure this was not in vain; our songs, our tales, our victory of incomprehensible weight, our suffering, this we will not give up for some plug of tobacco![75]

Iurii Bondarev was as absolute in his presentation at the Writers' Congress:

> If we don't stop the destruction of architectural monuments, if we don't stop the violence being done to the earth and rivers, if there is no moral explosion in science and in criticism, then one fine morning, which shall be our last and funeral morning, we shall awake with our undying optimism to learn that the national culture of vast Russia has been effaced, has vanished forever, is dead, destroyed and gone, along with its spirit, its beauty, its great literature, painting, and philosophy, while we sit naked and poor in the ashes, trying to remember the native alphabet which once was dear to our hearts, unable to do so because thought and feeling and joy and historical memory will all have disappeared.[76]

It is of course a modern fashion, at least in countries with powerful mass media, to complain of the degeneration of language, but in the Soviet case the complaints have at least in part a distinctly racial, or nationalist, undertone, as may be seen in comments by S. Danilov, the head of the Yakut Writers' Union—who is a Russian:

> Every year the flood of books written in a grey distilled Russian increases. Of late the national [i.e., non-Russian] authors are beginning to

take active part in this too. Having scarcely mastered elementary conversational Russian and textbook grammar, they consider it their duty to "enrich" Russian literature with their nasty little books.[77]

Nor does the racial subtext in this debate over language, history, and culture always remain only implicit, which suggests that the debate could get very much uglier in the future. Kunitsyn, for example, minces no words:

> We are all behind the "white wall" [meaning the limewashed walls of a church] of our great culture. Our ancestors once repulsed the onslaughts of the "unclean" by hiding behind white walls. These white stone walls served as their defense against invaders from the east and from the west . . . and so even today those same white spiritual walls, raised to glory and our salvation by our great countrymen, will preserve us.[78]

Even more open racism is apparent in a story by Viktor Astaf'ev, which caused a small scandal at the Writers' Congress when the Georgian delegates protested its publication as offensive to them. Although other delegates protested that, in Rasputin's words, "there was no offense being directed at the Georgian people" (Rasputin went on: "Read Astaf'ev's story more closely, dear Georgian comrades, and you will be able to distinguish pain from mockery and truth from lies"),[79] it is difficult to believe that passages such as the following from Astaf'ev's story were not designed to wound:

> There was something unpleasant in Otar's face and behavior. Where and when had he learned this lordly manner? Or had he been one way when we were in school together and now was another way in Georgia, resembling that boring type which the tongue doesn't even want to call Georgian. Like some sort of chopped, splintery shoot on the tree of humanity, this type pops up at every Russian bazaar, even in Murmansk and Noril'sk, contemptuously fleecing the credulous northern folk with rotten fruit and crushed, half-dead flowers. Greedy and unlettered, from those whom Russia calls "penny souls,"this type is everywhere seen unbuttoned to the waist, his pockets stuffed full and shining from his unwashed hands; he flings money about everywhere but cheese-pares with his wife, children, and parents. He is infected with motormania and grovels before imported goods, which is probably why he carts his fat children about, to show off their fashions, so that in all the hotels you can see some asthmatic, eight-year-old, 140-pound Gogi stuffed into jeans, his sleepy eyes drowning in his greasy cheeks.[80]

Glasnost' and the future

To anticipate the future, it is difficult to imagine how these various tensions might be eased in a single, unified cultural model, particularly since they are not mutually exclusive and so can augment one another. To increase the Great Russian influence in culture is to alienate the non-Russian, who not only has equal legal rights to the benefits of Soviet life but also, and more importantly, is increasingly the person upon whom the Soviet Union must rest in the future; not only are there going to be more non-Russians than Russians in the future USSR, but they are also going to be younger, less debilitated by drink and substance abuse, and more apt to have the psychological advantages that derive from firm family and cultural structures. To insist upon a model of high (and implicitly Russian) culture will also be to lose the greater part of adults and virtually all the young, not of course to rebellion, but simply to inattention. At the same time, to stress an all-Union and mass culture will outrage and alienate a powerful, articulate, and influential Russian minority, which the regime probably can not afford to do, and which in any event it would not do.

What seems likely then, as well as logical, is that the Soviet Union will begin to manifest some of the culture diversity that market forces have created in the West, by a distorted version of the same process. That is, youth must of necessity be reached and motivated, so ways will have to be found to put the desired message in a form that youth will receive. This would presumably mean jazzier television, more car chases in the movies, greater attention to fashion, and some attempt to, at best, make music a useful social tool or, more realistically, to disarm it as an agent of disaffection. The brutes of low culture must also be contained somehow, which would presumably result in much the same sort of cultural products as would the attempt to involve youth—better movies, more entertaining reading, and more amenities such as cafés and clothes, so that people could feel that reward and recreation are somehow possible outside of narcotism.

Finally, the link between nationalism and high culture will have to be more formally recognized, especially for the Russians. It is an irony of the Soviet Union that nationalities other than the Russian have been able to retain or reappropriate a good deal of their own pasts, because the Revolution was not a specific repudiation of their national cultures. For the Russians, though, the Revolution was a specific rejection of the Russian church, the Russian monarchy, Russian agriculture, and Russian social organization; since in the early days the Bolsheviks assaulted even the language, it is not too far-fetched to say that the target of the Revolution was Russia itself. Now, seventy years later, other nationalities can take pride in their heritage yet remain loyal Soviet citizens in ways that Russians who seek to celebrate their "Russianness" cannot, since they quickly will come to seem anti-Soviet, as can be seen in the hesitant delicacy with which Gorbachev's officials are handling the emergence of the extremely nationalist, unofficial group memory. It seems logical then that the authorities will have to recognize this imbalance, by continuing to publish Nabokov, Gumilev, and other artifacts of past culture, by better preserving architectural monuments, and perhaps even by reaching some *modus vivendi* with Orthodoxy (for which the millennial celebration in 1989 might provide a natural opportunity), to somehow separate the desirable strands of nationalism from the unwanted ones of religion.

The mechanism of this relationship, in which the government would attempt to make some virtue of necessity by adapting to its purposes practices in which the people are engaging anyway, seems almost certainly to be the mechanism of the whole Gorbachev "thaw,"which ought logically to permit us to assume that *glasnost'*, greater latitude in the arts, and a generally more diverse cultural life will continue to grow. Unfortunately, there is an equally possible course, since there is every evidence, in this stage of that long post-Zhdanov thaw and in earlier ones, that bureaucratic instincts for routine, secrecy, and putting a good face on things are tremendously strong. In the interests of keeping things "as they are," the authorities might equally well proceed against what would seem to be their own long-term interests, in the attempt to demonstrate, as First Secretary of the Writers' Union V. Karpov put it, that "Soviet literature has firmly held and will continue to hold its Soviet and Party positions."[81] In that case literature, and culture more generally, would presumably be forced to return to the wooden masquerades of the past. If that should happen, the task for western analysts would become more difficult again, because it will increase the discrepancies between the cultural artifacts available to us and those the Soviet people *in fact* enjoy, but there is little evidence that the Soviet people will not continue to do what they are doing, regardless. That is, it seems wholly likely that the processes of Soviet culture outlined above will continue of their own accord, in great part independent of higher control; the tempo of development can be influenced by decisions of the authorities, but its basic directions (which are various) will remain as they have been outlined here.

Based upon the evidence available, the Soviet people seem to be increasingly turned inward, concentrating on the self and the family, and paying only the minimum of heed necessary to the larger concerns of the nation. This inwardness will force the government to calculate much better how it is to catch public attention and so engage its people in the life of the nation. Although it would seem in the best interests of the regime to continue its present tactics of permitting artists, editors, writers, and film-makers to seek audiences with the qualities and subjects of their work, the authorities equally plausibly could return to their former, more browbeating cultural ways. In either event, it would seem that the one thing the long post-Zhdanov climb will have taught the Soviet people is that in the essentially private decisions that in sum define a people's culture, it is the government which must eventually come to them, and not the other way about.

Notes

1. See the account of Meilakh's arrest and conviction in *Zvezda*, 1985 (3).
2. *Literaturnaia gazeta*, 23 July 1986, 2.
3. FBIS, USSR, 16 December 1986, R5.
4. *Literaturnaia gazeta*, 2 July 1986, 6.
5. *Literaturnaia gazeta*, 14 May 1986, 7.
6. *Literaturnaia gazeta*, 12 March 1986, 11.
7. *Neva*, 1986 (3), 135.
8. *Znamia*, 1986 (6).
9. *Literaturnaia gazeta*, 2 July 1986, 7.
10. V. Rasputin, "The Fire," *Soviet Literature*, 1986 (7), 45.
11. *Literaturnaia gazeta*, 2 July 1986, 9.
12. V. Astaf'ev, "Pechal'nyi detektiv," *Oktiabr'*, 1986 (1), 25–26.
13. *Ibid.*, 73.
14. *Literaturnaia gazeta*, 13 August 1986, 4.
15. I. Kryvelev, "Koketnichaia s bozhenkoi," *Komsomol'skaia pravda*, 30 July 1986, 4.
16. *Nash sovremennik*, 1986 (1), 176.
17. In his RSFSR Writers' Union speech, incompletely quoted in *Literaturnaia gazeta*, 18 December 1985, 5.
18. *Literaturnaia gazeta*, 30 July 1986, 4.
19. *Literaturnaia gazeta*, 23 July 1986, 2.
20. *Literaturnaia gazeta*, 2 July 1986, 6.
21. N. Miroshnichenko, "Chitaiushchaia? Ili tantsuiushchaia?" *Literaturnaia Rossiia*, 21 November 1986, 15.
22. A. Shestopalov, *Obshchenie: vozmozhnost' i deistvitel'nost'*, Frunze, 1986, 158–161.
23. *Literaturnaia gazeta*, 25 June 1986, 11.
24. See for example V. Mushtaev, "Efirnyi defitsit," *Literaturnaia Rossiia*, 18 July 1986.

25. See for example G. Iakovlev, "Literatura po instruktsii," *Literaturnaia Rossiia*, 24 January 1986, 3.

26. N. Katerli, "Polina," *Neva*, 1984 (1), 36.

27. V. Kardin, "Sekret uspekha," *Voprosy literatury*, 1986 (4), 107.

28. *Literaturnaia gazeta*, 23 July 1986, 3.

29. *Literaturnaia gazeta*, 23 July 1986, 3.

30. *Literaturnaia gazeta*, 23 July 1986, 2.

31. *Literaturnaia gazeta*, 23 July 1986, 7.

32. *Literaturnaia Rossiia*, 21 November 1986, 8.

33. See for example A. Rybakov, "Bez grubykh slov," *Literaturnaia gazeta*, 17 September 1986, 3. Rybakov cites a number of "horrors," among them a wide-eyed, well-satisfied American girl who pants to her Russian lover, "With you I don't have a body, I have a . . . a . . . an I don't know what. Some kind of knot of bliss. And now I am an entire orchestra, and you are the conductor."

34. B. Metal'nikov, "Ekran zhizni," *Literaturnaia gazeta*, 21 May 1986, 8.

35. A. Tumanian, *Literaturnaia gazeta*, 23 July 1986, 8.

36. "Ne prishli i ne skazali," *Literaturnaia gazeta*, 16 July 1986, 8.

37. *Literaturnaia gazeta*, 2 July 1986, 6.

38. Iu. Gladil'shchikov, "Nostalgia po muzeiu," *Literaturnaia gazeta*, 20 August 1986, 8.

39. L. Korsunskii, "Nuzhnaia tema," *Literaturnaia gazeta*, 26 March 1986, 8.

40. V. Golovanov, "Slovno rok nad etim rokom," *Literaturnaia gazeta*, 15 October 1986, 8

41. "Eshche raz o roke," *Sobesednik*, 2 August 1986, 5.

42. I. Sinitsyn, "Delo slavy," *Nash sovremennik*, 1986 (1).

43. *Ibid.*, 7.

44. *Neva*, 1986 (1), 114.

45. N. Katerli, "Tsvetnye otkrytki," *Neva*, 1986 (5), 70.

46. *Literaturnaia gazeta*, 20 August 1986, 4.

47. *Literaturnaia gazeta*, 13 August 1986, 4.

48. A. Anan'ev, "Seredina puti," *Oktiabr'*, 1986 (3), 7.

49. *Literaturnaia gazeta*, 23 July 1986, 3.

50. See for example Ul'mas Umarbekov's comments in *Literaturnaia gazeta*, 2 July 1986, 5.

51. G. Sorokin, "Groza nad Kizhami," *Literaturnaia gazeta*, 9 April 1986, 12.

52. *Literaturnaia gazeta*, 26 June 1986, 12.

53. *Literaturnaia gazeta*, 26 March 1986, 12.

54. *Literaturnaia gazeta*, 2 July 1986, 9.

55. *Pravda*, 20 August 1986, 1.

56. *Radio Liberty Research Bulletin* (RL 277/86), 17 July 1986, 7.

57. *Literaturnaia gazeta*, 23 July 1986, 3.

58. These were the same children who were asked to name their heroes (see above); Sinitsyn, *op. cit.*, 5.

59. *Literaturnaia gazeta*, 30 July 1986, 8.

60. *Literaturnaia Rossiia*, 14 November 1986, 6.

61. FBIS Daily Report/USSR, 9 December 1986, R 4.

62. *Literaturnaia Rossiia*, 31 October 1986, 2.

63. *Literaturnaia gazeta*, 23 July 1986, 3.

64. *Novyi mir*, No. 1, 1986.

65. *Komsomol'skaia pravda*, 10 December 1986, 2.

66. *Literaturnaia Rossiia*, 21 November 1986, 3.

67. Evtushenko, *op. cit.*

68. *Komsomol'skaia pravda*, 10 December 1986, 2.

69. Ch. Aitmatov, "Plakha," *Novyi mir*, 1986 (9), 48.

70. *Ibid.*, 47.

71. *Literaturnaia gazeta*, 16 July 1986, 2.

72. V. Lakshin, "O dome i o mire," *Literaturnoe obozrenie*, 1981 (10), 40.

73. I. Kryvelev, "Koketnichaia s bozhenkoi," *Komsomol'skaia pravda*, 30 July 1986, 4.

74. *Literaturnaia gazeta*, 2 July 1986, 6.

75. Kunitsyn, *op. cit.*

76. *Literaturnaia gazeta*, 2 July 1986, 4.

77. *Literaturnaia Rossiia*, 31 October 1986, 3.

78. Kunitsyn, *op. cit.*, 182.

79. *Literaturnaia gazeta*, 2 July 1986, 10.

80. V. Astaf'ev, "Mesto deistviia," *Nash sovremennik*, 1986 (5), 125.

81. *Literaturnaia gazeta*, 26 November 1986, 1.

MAKING THE MEDIA WORK:
SOVIET SOCIETY AND COMMUNICATIONS

Ellen Mickiewicz

Introduction

Under Mikhail Gorbachev the Soviet mass media have undergone significant change. In part, this is a result of trends that have been developing over the last decade, but it is also a result of policies initiated by the new leader. It is perhaps in this area that Gorbachev has effected the most dramatic changes—considerably more far-reaching than those that have been enacted in the economy, the educational system, and other sectors of Soviet society. The first part of this essay looks at the trends in the media system itself, particularly in terms of the revolutionary impact of television. This new medium, with its capacity to transmit uniform messages with unheard-of rapidity to the largest mass public in Soviet history—virtually the entire population—has created a new communications reality. Because the press has been treated at length in a number of published works, in the Soviet Union and in the West, it is not analyzed here. Its importance in the Soviet media system is, obviously, very great, but we must remember that the readership of the national newspapers is decisively skewed toward the well educated and the politically active. Therefore, newspapers can be said to tap only a fraction of the huge and heterogeneous (in terms of level of education, age, sex, and place of residence) audience for television.

The second part of the essay looks at specific societal questions on which the media have had a significant impact. Most of these questions

Ellen Mickiewicz is professor of political science at Emory University.

have not, as yet, been studied. The final section examines the complex and contradictory impact that is likely to result.

The changing media system

In 1940 there were only 400 television sets in the Soviet Union; in 1950, 10,000; in 1960, 4.8 million. Then in the five years between 1965 and 1980, the previous pattern of growth changed, and the availability of television sets more than doubled. With a crash program, the production of television sets jumped in the '70s, and by 1976, Soviet industry was producing seven million sets annually, most in black-and-white.[1] The production of color television sets has been increasing and will soon account for a majority of new sets. But the color sets continue to be plagued by poor quality control and a significant number of them are prone to explode and catch fire. In fact, the fire in Moscow's Hotel Rossiia was blamed on just such an event. New calls have gone out for improvements in production.

By 1986 fully 93 percent of the population had access to television and it covered more than 86 percent of the territory of the USSR—an enormous jump from the 5 percent of the population able to watch television in 1960.[2] Of the roughly twenty million who do not yet receive television programs, all but two million are rural residents, most scattered in sparsely inhabited regions of Siberia.[3] Although the political leaders were undoubtedly slow to grasp the potential of television to capture the attention of the population, and, therefore, to function as an important instrument of persuasion, equally critical was the configuration of the country itself. The Soviet Union's huge land mass stretches over eleven time zones, and it would be impossibly expensive to create a true television network without communications satellites. But, with communications satellites, that sprawling, inhospitable territory can be leapfrogged and signals beamed down at relatively low cost. Communications satellites have radically altered information diffusion in the Soviet Union.[4] In record time a major new medium of communication has been placed in homes across a vast and linguistically differentiated country. For the first time a mass public has been created, as the new electronic medium transmits its messages directly to an enormous number of individuals who receive it outside the structures of organized groups. Television communicates with unprecedented rapidity and reach. News and information that the government wishes to transmit will, because of the technical capability and the viewing habits of audiences, almost instantaneously spread across the country in a single approved version. Moreover, the audience considers that version far more credible than any produced by other media. As Soviet television expert E. G. Bagirov noted, "in the credibility of the display of events, it [television] has no equal."[5] The world, especially the West, now comes to the Soviet people mainly from the television screen.[6] It should have been foreseen that significant changes would be wrought by such a sudden shift in the way people learn about the world, but the effects of this new medium were, to a large extent, unplanned. As we shall see below, there have been contradictory effects: some are likely to pose problems for the regime in the years ahead, at the same time that others reinforce regime policies. Untangling these paradoxes will be part of the later discussion.

The media form a system of interrelated components. The mass media are usually taken to include newspapers, magazines, television, radio, and film. In the Soviet Union, the term *mass media* (or the more usual "media of mass information and propaganda"—SMIP is the Russian acronym) is sometimes expanded to include theater and even book publishing. Increasingly, in the Gorbachev era, SMI is used, dropping "propaganda" from the term. Additionally, in the Soviet Union there is a system of oral mass media (SMUP: media of mass oral propaganda), which includes the heavily attended lectures by the "Znanie" (Knowledge) Society, as well as the various forms of political information and agitation, including party education.[7] The functionality of the oral media system vis-à-vis the rapidly developing mass media has become problematic. That mass media system has itself undergone radical change since the introduction of television.

The effect of television on radio

When one part of a system of communications changes dramatically, it is reasonable to assume that the other parts of the system will be affected. In the United States, the introduction of television had its most powerful effect on radio; both its audience and function have changed substantially. This is a logical development, since the characteristics of radio and television are most closely associated. Both can constitute secondary activity: one can listen to radio or watch television while doing something else, whereas newspaper reading demands more undivided attention. Moreover, radio and television require much less highly developed cognitive skills than does newspaper reading. It is simpler for the less educated to get their information from listening or viewing; reading is much more difficult, particularly for many of the older people in the Soviet Union, who are more likely to belong to the generation that had not yet benefited from the growing embrace of the general educational system. Both radio and television can be received in the home, unlike movies, and the Soviet film industry registered a decline in box office receipts when television was introduced. Theater ticket sales have dropped as well, with theaters only half full, on the average, nationwide.

Radio is not what it once was. Not long ago, an article ran in *Literaturnaia gazeta* complaining about "screaming loudspeakers" carrying radio programs to outdoor public places. The article conveyed the complaints of a number of letter-writers from various parts of the country. It is not only the noise level that was objectionable, but, more important, the very function of the public dissemination of radio broadcasts for informational purposes was now called obsolete. As the correspondent writes: "In the '30s to listen to radio . . . at all was a pleasure . . . [it was received as] a miracle. . . . In the thinking of some officials, . . . the idea of radio holds the same place in the culture it did decades ago. But radio has a different role today. . . . It's time to revise our attitude toward radio as a medium of mass communication."[8] A survey published in 1981 (but carried out in the late '70s) found that urban male workers listen to the radio only 9 minutes a day on the average. Female workers listen 5 minutes a day. Male white-collar technical specialists listen 11 minutes a day; female, only 3 minutes.[9]

A very different assessment was made late in 1985 by the deputy director of Gosteleradio, who asserted that radio is on the rebound, with the average urbanite tuning in more than one and a half hours a day. He credits this growth to the development of small radio sets, higher consumption of automobiles (equipped with radios), and the introduction of stereo sound.[10] If this figure is correct, or even partially correct, it represents an unusual turnaround. The anomalous revival of a component of the larger media system is an important phenomenon, one that should be explored seriously.

Increased automobile ownership cannot account for all of the rise in listening. Certainly it is important, especially for the weather reports that drivers depend on. But there are not enough automobiles on the road to account for the radio listening figure. The availability of more sophisticated, cheaper, and more portable sets also accounts for a portion of the increase in the rate of radio listening, but there may well be another factor.

Changes in programming may have attracted—or rather reattracted —an audience. To the extent that radio took advantage, before television did, of an easing of program guidelines; to the extent that radio programming became more lively, more information oriented (including information about the West), it was able to widen its audience. In particular, the news and music program "Maiak" (Beacon), started in 1964, has successfully brought back to radio listening a population of students, young workers, and scientific and technical specialists. It is the transmitting of relatively fast-breaking news, both foreign and domestic, and heavy programming of more up-to-date pop music that has attracted a growing audience.[11]

Until the very recent revival of radio, the radio audience was, in sociological terms, overaged, undereducated, and low-income.[12] The new audience is likely to be upscale (especially if ownership of a car is involved) in terms of education and income—in short, a very different audience.

The potential of radio is, however, constricted by what appears to be lack of clarity about the specificity of function of each of the components of the mass media system. Although there is, on paper, a method by which all of the components of the media system are coordinated, the statements of those in charge do not indicate an appreciation—or rather, sufficient appreciation—of the distinctiveness of each medium. As one official, the chairman of the Saratov branch of Gosteleradio, said in response to a question about how his organization gives orders for the division of themes between radio and television: "I would say that there is no division, but there is a considered distribution of questions on one and the same theme."[13] Practitioners and local administrators do not share a clear common understanding of the specificities of the components of the media system, and the theoretical literature does not provide much guidance. A new book on the media system states that radio has its advantages and distinguishing characteristics: "the spoken word and the acoustically realistic picture . . . permits direct transmission and a practically limitless audience." It enjoys "ubiquity, maximal timeliness (including what happens this very minute) [and] always increasing frequency of broadcasts."[14] But "in the scheme of the entire representation of relations among people—the portrayal of man in the grand scheme—television has the advantage in comparison with the press and radio."[15]

Radio's ability to carry fast-breaking news (defined in Soviet terms) is relatively recent. In the past, radio broadcasters depended on *Pravda* for their news agendas, and it was only in 1960 that a resolution of the Central Committee directed radio to broadcast news before it appeared in the newspaper.[16] "Maiak" broadcasts news at least twice an hour, and altogether, taking into account all of the broadcasts over the national radio networks, there are 88 news broadcasts daily, for a total volume of 24 hours and 42 minutes.[17] But the evening news market is dominated by television.[18]

These significant changes in the pattern of radio listening, although they do not and will not interfere with the preeminence of television, do suggest a much greater official understanding of audience demands. At the same time, it is insufficiently understood that functional differentiation of the electronic media—and all media for that matter—would further strengthen the regime's quest for efficacy.

Videotape recorders

The videotape recorder is an example of the dilemma created by the rapid development of information sources that are made portable and versatile by technology. In the case of VCRs the Soviet leadership is concerned not only about the economic issues (the flourishing of black market enterprises) and the moral issues involved (the distribution of sexually explicit and hedonistic materials to a protected population), but also about the political implications. In the press, they have made a connection between the importation of contraband cassettes and what they deem a Western effort to undermine the Soviet regime. Pornography, a recent article said, "is interwoven with lauding the bourgeois way of life. It goes without saying that this, too, is aimed primarily at poisoning the mind of the younger generation."[19]

The dilemma for the Soviet leadership is located in the lagging production of domestic cassettes and the relatively easy and uncontrollable availability of contraband tapes. Although domestic production of VCRs and tapes is still very slow, official concern may be seen in the plan for growth in the coming years. About 4,000 VCRs a year have been produced in recent years, but that figure is set by the plan to increase to 60,000 in 1990 and 120,000 in 2000. Many VCRs have come back with journalists and diplomats; others are imported, though the question of format compatability makes it more difficult: the Soviets use the French SECAM system. Still, the shortage is enormous, relative to demand.

As for videocassettes, the first rental store in the country was started in Voronezh, where the Soviet-made vcr is produced. Until late in 1985, it was the only such store, but now they exist in Moscow and are slated to appear in all republic capitals and many port cities.[20] The stock of cassettes available for rent is still very small for a population of over 280 million people. In mid–1985, there were only 250 officially produced cassettes in distribution, although the number was to double by the end of that year and continue rapidly upward thereafter. The failure to anticipate this newest spinoff of the television revolution (a recurring problem as Soviet policy-makers confront an exploding information revolution) has resulted in a rush of illegal imports to fill the void. This out-of-control influx of cassettes is bringing in pornography and films the regime objects to on political grounds, such as "Rocky IV" and "Rambo." This has become known through the very well publicized arrests and trials of underground entrepreneurs. The black market seems to have no geographical limitations, and the scale is sometimes very large, as, for example, the ring in Riga, which, when raided by the police, yielded 415 tapes.[21] The ring in Tashkent specialized in Bruce Lee films and pornography and went from village to village showing the tapes to audiences of 15 men at a time. A Moscow ring was the most sophisticated reported: it employed a staff of translators (many from prestigious institutes) and sold cassettes and video equipment. One-and-a-half to 3½ years in prison is an often cited punishment for "video speculation." In an attempt to assert control over the flow of unofficial videotapes, new legislation was enacted making a criminal offense the "making, storing, distribution, or showing of films propagating the 'cult of violence and cruelty,'" a crime subject to imprisonment for up to two years.[22] This August 1986 addition to the Russian Republic's criminal code serves as a model for the other republics.

The phenomenon of vcr acquisition and tape distribution demonstrates certain important consequences of the media revolution in the Soviet Union. First, information boundaries are porous, and although security officials have attempted to control the illegal trade, they will have only limited success. Second, the regime had underestimated interest in and ease of transmission of the new technology. To some extent, by rapidly creating a dense network of television sets across the country, they are themselves responsible for the demand for the spinoffs of television. Third, as in other aspects of the television revolution that we shall see below, the activism of the West is at issue. The more aggressive information policies of the Reagan administration are cited repeatedly in connection with the penetration of national borders. Fourth, it is unlikely that even with a crash program, the demand can be satisfied. We should look for adaptation in some other fashion, as, for example, increased use of clubs to coopt or preempt the activity insofar as possible or reevaluation of Komsomol activities to wrest this activity away from the black market sector.

Social issues and media effectiveness

The influence of the new electronic medium, television, is said by Soviet officialdom to be very great. In fact, television is credited with the decisive influence on career choice among young people. The deputy director of Gosteleradio, G. K. Iushkiavichius, states that *some 70 percent* of the young people today chose their occupations because of television.[23] The extent to which television functions as a determinant of social stratification is, as yet, unstudied, but it is clearly a key variable in understanding social and occupational mobility. In order to analyze this, it is essential to look at the occupational spread portrayed on television as well as the manner in which individual occupations are treated. Television itself may have become a high status occupation. In the popular film "Moscow Does Not Believe in Tears," which was a catalogue of modern social trends, one of the leading characters—he is distinguished by his proclivity for following trends—boasts that the future is in television. There will only be television, he says, no books, no plays. At the Moscow University School of Journalism, the most prestigious in the country, interest in television journalism has increased so much that a new competition has been instituted. Students admitted to the school who wish to specialize in television have to take three additional examinations: oral presentation in front of the camera; improvisation of commentary; and creation of a literary portrait.[24]

There are other dimensions to career choice. There is a weekly program designed not only to inculcate military/patriotic values and positively present the draft obligation, but also to reinforce the image of the military as a career. What precisely are the dimensions of this service that are chosen for portrayal? How are other jobs depicted? Can television, if properly utilized, help to reallocate positions in the stratification scheme?

Television is also credited with reducing labor turnover. It is said to have been essential to the creation of the Baikal-Amur Rail Line, in enabling the workers to adapt to the harsh climate and lack of leisure time options. To what extent is or can television be harnessed to economic development?

In the early days of television in the Soviet Union, signals emanating from the center had a limited range. It became the practice for local studios to transmit their own messages, in the absence of programs from Moscow. Many of these were in indigenous languages. The contribution of local television studios went into decline about 12 to 15 years ago, according to Iushkiavichius. He attributed the decline to the fact that "the ideological-artistic level and the technical equipment of local TV were lower than on Central Television."[25] That may be only part of the complex administrative problem of those days. Because of central concern about the centrifugal pull of the ethnic minorities, a more centralized direction of programming was decreed in 1970, when television was placed before radio in the title of the governmental administrative body overseeing the two media—Gosteleradio, the State Committee for Television and Radio Broadcasting.[26] The reorganization strengthened party control not only over national, but also over local broadcasting. The intermediate link between the individual studios and the center was abolished and a central administration for local broadcasting was established.

Television is said to have a powerful centralizing and integrating force in societies where it is widely diffused. Certainly the integration of ethnic minorities (including linguistic assimilation) and the consequent reduction of communal tendencies would be a very desirable effect of television from the point of view of the regime. First Program, the older and more prestigious of the national networks, has a large national audience; Second Program has an audience less than half its size. Localities may add channels (for example, Moscow has two more and receives Leningrad's channel as well). Local programming is often transmitted in "windows" in the national networks, and usually it is Second Program that is preempted. The authors of the Taganrog survey, Grushin and Onikov, remark that in Rostov Oblast, local television takes over 4½ hours of Second Program (8:00–11:00 p.m.).[27] There are complaints that local programming is amateurish and excessively devoted to dull programs on agriculture and industry. In Taganrog, there was a proposal to construct a city television studio. A survey of opinion there found that respondents agreed that local television and radio broadcasts paid too little attention to events in their city, but they were by no means in agreement that a city television studio would be an improvement. Almost half of those surveyed opposed construction of the studio, arguing that there was a more critical need for housing construction and improvement in public services and that the new programs would probably not be of much interest, since they were likely to concentrate on economic production. As one respondent commented: "Really, if there are hardly any interesting programs coming from the province studio, what can you expect from the city!"[28]

The ability of television to be a powerful integrating force may differ according to the level of education of the viewer. Television creates the most heterogeneous public in history. The newspaper public is relatively highly educated, in comparison with national averages. The college educated constitute disproportionately large shares of the readership of the major newspapers: for *Literaturnaia gazeta*, three-fourths, for *Pravda* about two-fifths, for *Izvestiia* one-half, and for *Trud* one-fourth. Television, on the other hand, does not depend on highly developed cognitive skills and draws an audience that ranges from the barely literate rural viewer to the academician in Moscow. It may be argued, moreover, that it has brought into the range of official messages those who had previously been left out. Television's greatest impact may be on these people, the information-poor, a finding that is not unlike that found in studies of American television audiences: "television news increases information levels more among less-educated respondents than among better educated respondents."[29] This suggests that it would be a mistake to confine our understanding of the effects of television in the Soviet Union only to those who have access to and systematically utilize a large number of other information sources (including foreign information sources) in addition to television. We should keep in mind, too, that the levels of education in the Soviet Union are far lower than in the United States—about 40 percent of the rural and 20 percent of the urban population have not gone beyond the fourth grade.

There are some hints, however, that television's virtually magnetic attraction for the poorly educated (and, in general, the poor, who have little income to spend on other leisure time options) may result in *limiting* opportunities for upward mobility for these "addicts." The commitment to passive consumption and the resulting unwillingness to engage in improvement of one's qualifications by attending night and correspondence schools and other forms of active advancement might actually exacerbate class differences. As with most complex social phenomena, it is probably the case that both of these functions operate simultaneously, which should alert us to the necessity to ponder with some care the contradictory impact of the media system as a whole and its newest entrant, television, in particular.

Agenda-setting and international issues

Over the course of several years the Soviet media system as a whole, not only television, has been remarkably successful in mobilizing the attention of the media public to foreign, particularly Western, political systems. There is a very high (some officials now say disproportionately high) level of attention to the West in the Soviet media. A survey of *Pravda* found that it devoted about 44 percent of its international stories to the United States and its allies, while Soviet-type systems were given about 31 percent.[30] Soviet television news is heavily focused on the West, and in non-news programming—from movies to youth shows— the West, particularly America, is at the center of attention. We have a good deal of information on how salient the West is for the Soviet media public, and much of it comes from studies of newspaper readership. What the studies show is a thirst for information about the world outside the Soviet Union. This thirst, which officials regard with some concern, is probably, paradoxically, the result of official Soviet policy. In every survey of newspaper readers, whether of national or local papers, the strong preference for international stories is both consistent and stable over time. Most readers turn first to stories about international events, and this interest cuts across all age groups, all levels of education, and all occupations. Even the readers of *Trud,* the daily with the lowest proportion of college-educated readers, when asked to identify the area they like more information about, cited international news first. Other areas of newspaper coverage (science, technology, culture, economics, family, youth, etc.) exhibit differences in readership by education, or other variables, that international stories do not.[31] In a 1973 survey by *Literaturnaia gazeta,* it was found that fully 88 percent of the subscribers were attentive to the section ''International Life.'' This was the most popular subject. In last place were stories on national liberation movements and the Third World; stories on fellow socialist countries ranked next to last.[32] It is the capitalist countries that attract the greatest interest. To be sure, newspaper and television stories tend to be negative, containing accusations of aggressive policies of imperialism or depictions of the crises of capitalism—but they do dominate foreign news. In the spring of 1986, *Pravda* printed an article calling for more varied coverage of the United States, including positive sides.

In practice, these more upbeat stories, like one on the McDonald's fast food chain, would function as examples of economic initiative that could be applied to the Soviet economy.

The central importance of coverage of the West is very clear, and concern is voiced that things may have gone too far. One such opinion stated that "the clear, deep demonstration of the strengths of the world system of socialism, of the camp of democracy and progress, should occupy the leading place among articles on international questions."[33] By focusing so intensely on the nature of the adversary, this warning implies, the Soviet media may encourage interest in the West, perhaps too much. The strong preference the public exhibits for international and particularly Western news has become a source of apprehension. Official coverage of the West, which has been so massive, is designed to strengthen support by focusing on a constant and pervasive threat from the West. That another consequence as well has ensued—a virtual thirst for news of the West—appears to be an unintended consequence. The very mobilization of the public has clearly created interest in unofficial sources of information. If unwelcome instrusions of unofficial and unapproved information (whether via foreign radio broadcasts, tourists, the increasing numbers of professional journals, or reception of foreign television in border regions such as the Baltic republics) were a fact of life, then they had to be countered, but effectively—and to be effective, the media had to go some part of the way in meeting audience demands. It is a dilemma of control and effectiveness in constant tension. It is this tension that is central to the twin policies of *glasnost'* and *operativnost'*—watchwords of Gorbachev's media policies.

Glasnost' and *operativnost'*
(openness and timeliness)

Timeliness, or rapid response time, has not, traditionally, been of any great importance to Soviet media. In their understanding of what is newsworthy, the fact that an event occurred in the previous 24 hours was of little consequence. What Marxist doctrine told Soviet media officials was that news is made by that which reveals or documents the underlying reality toward which history is tending. Since history is seen in its Marxist-Leninist interpretation, that means that the reality toward which history is moving is already known. The "reality" of antisocial or retrograde events (for example, strikes and crime in socialist countries, sensationalism, etc.) is ephemeral; these things will pass as communism is attained. On the other hand, stories about improvements in harvesting operations or the introduction of new machines are considered newsworthy, since, although hardly fast-breaking news, they represent movement along the way to the economy of the future. Moreover, such stories help to fulfill the primary mission of the media, which is to socialize or mold the population by holding up models for emulation.

But much is changing in this comfortable formulation. Soviet media officials understand, in a way they had not before, the complex interaction between message and receiver. The old "hypodermic effects" model, though still employed occasionally, is no longer thought to be operative. According to this model, the transmission of a communication is synonymous with its assimilation. Saturating a population with repetitive messages guarantees persuasion.[34] This assumption, which dominated Soviet communication theory (and, at one time, Western communication theory as well) has lost most of its authority. Soviet officialdom has also been increasingly aware of the importance of being the first to transmit information. The source breaking the story is more effective in setting the agenda; counterpersuasion is more difficult, because it is more difficult to change predispositions and attitudes than to activate them. Thus, more information must be provided (*glasnost'*)—and rapidly (*operativnost'*). The average citizen is in a much better position to judge coverage on domestic matters than on international events. Newspapers and television, particularly the local newspaper, are not the only sources of information; people know about the things around them through observation and through word of mouth from relatives and friends. There are multiple sources of information and the ability to verify independently. In this situation the news medium operates with less credibility if it either fails to cover events that are known about and taken seriously, or covers them in a superficial or unrealistic way. Because of the policy of simply avoiding stories that will disturb people, the credibility of the local media is very low. People say they won't read articles even on subjects that interest them.[35] Nor do they find enough information about subjects they care about: they can't find much about crime or about shopping, public services, and city planning. What they do see is full of errors. According to one report, 97 percent of the readers of a district newspaper of a city found it usually distorted the events it described. Because of the prohibition on stories about deviance and because their mission is to socialize readers in a single acceptable fashion, local papers present a view of life that is unreal and stilted. Television at the local level is no more attractive. The closer the medium is to the lives of the people to whom it is addressed, the greater the opportunity to evaluate the coverage independently.[36] And stories that go unreported do not evaporate.

Soviet officials now appear to wish to take back the ground they have ceded to word of mouth and hearsay. The new call for openness and timeliness has gone out strongly and with much publicity under Gorbachev, but it had started before. In 1983, an article in *Pravda* commented on experiments in the use of television in the republic of Georgia:

> Suppose that a railroad accident occurred at 12:00 noon in some district. The "grapevine" reports such incidents quickly. Understanding well that such rumors are harmful, Georgian Television has made timeliness one of the most important principles of public affairs progams. As a result, that same evening you can tune in the regular "Today's Interview" series and hear the head of the railroad tell what's actually happening. . . . Georgian Television reporters probe the true state of affairs, help the viewers distinguish truth from gossip and try to deprive the magic formula "they say" of its power to charm.[37]

Yet clearly, the tempo and range of change have increased under Gorbachev. Drug use has been covered, letters are published that are more candid than in the past, attacking corruption, even among party officials (though *Pravda* was later criticized for taking this license). Several new call-in television programs subject officials to interrogation from consumers. The boldest and most innovative television program, "12th Floor," pits young people, who speak with unheard-of candor, against the bureaucracies that affect their lives, such as the Komsomol and the Ministry of Education. Young people, including even so-called "*metalisty*" (in American jargon, "metalheads," or fans of heavy metal rock groups) who would earlier have been attacked as dangerous proponents of the counterculture, have been treated sympathetically on television. But the most critical and important test of openness and timeliness was Chernobyl.

Coverage of Chernobyl is a clear line of demarcation signaling the new policy. It represents a radical departure from the past in its scope, though it must be seen as part of a developing policy that under crisis conditions was unexepectedly accelerated. It is the first and most serious test of the "new thinking" of the new regime. The Chernobyl coverage illustrates all of the new dimensions of Gorbachev's media policy: in part it was a call for an intensified work ethic in the form of contributions to the effort to deal with the disaster (from the volunteers who evacuated local residents to farmers who had to work harder to make up for the produce destroyed). In part it was a monitoring and control effort, as those who did not perform adequately were publicly stripped of their privileges and responsibilities. But most of all, it was an effort to build credibility for the media. After an initial and, as is openly acknowledged, damaging silence, there followed a depth and breadth of coverage unprecedented in Soviet media. That this coverage was not an aberration, but rather evidence of a new policy can be seen in the full and vivid coverage of a later disaster, the sinking of the cruise ship Admiral Nakhimov, and the unusual coverage given to the hijacking of a Soviet plane in Ufa and communal disorders in Alma-Ata—all in 1986.

Openness and timeliness are, in my view, of particular importance for domestic news and information, where, as I have indicated above, opportunities for independent verification are more widespread. However, the new Gorbachev policy can be seen in the international sphere as well. The motivation for change in this area is, according to Gorbachev and his predecessor, concern about the intrusiveness of Western messages, called by Chernenko an "information intervention" and by Gorbachev, "information imperialism."[38] Yet while the Gorbachev regime sees a threat and a challenge from the West's information campaign, it perceives a greater ability of the Soviet population to withstand its persuasive intent. It is likely that this confidence prompted Soviet propaganda chief Aleksandr Iakovlev to raise with the United States Information Agency head, Charles Wick, the proposal that jamming of the Voice of America be eliminated in return for access to American medium-wave facilities.[39] In fact, jamming of BBC and Voice of America broadcasts was lifted in 1987.

That ability to withstand persuasion does depend, however, on the level of interest in international issues, the degree to which the official media are trusted concerning these issues, and whether or not trusted alternative sources or opportunities for independent verification exist. On the first point, I have noted that the Soviet media themselves have been largely successful in setting the agenda; international or foreign issues, particularly involving the West, have become salient—perhaps too salient. On the second point, we do know that Soviet media enjoy considerably more trust and authority about international than about domestic issues, and, as communication theory tells us, it is both possible and routine for contradictions to coexist in individual cognitive schemas, so that confidence in official media may be low on local issues, while relatively high on other issues.[40] Finally, for most people, the ability to verify international news is very limited. The Afghanistan war, to the extent that it increasingly affects participants and the friends and families of participants, and is known about chiefly through hearsay, is surely a potentially dangerous counterpoise to official media policy. On most international issues, however, people's opportunities to arrive at counterinformation are constrained, particularly given the much greater persuasive power of the visuals of the television networks.

However, here, too, the source breaking the story has the distinct advantage, and clearly, Soviet media policy is in the process of change. There have been notable examples recently of openness and timeliness about international issues in the media. Even before Gorbachev came to power, there had been two press conferences—one given by then Foreign Minister Andrei Gromyko, and the remarkable one given by Marshal Ogarkov after the Korean Airlines plane was shot down. After Gorbachev became General Secretary, the institution of the press conference became virtually routine, used very frequently in the Chernobyl coverage. In Paris, in October 1985, Gorbachev held a press conference with President Mitterand that was broadcast both at home and abroad: earlier, he had met with French journalists in the Kremlin, and this, too, was broadcast at home and in Paris. These two press conferences were riddled with difficult and challenging questions, of the sort that the public had not heard before, but would hear again in the Donahue/Pozner space bridge. Charges of discrimination against Jews, questions about the treatment of political prisoners, the Sakharov case, and many other difficult issues were raised. By the end of that month an agreement had been reached which gave four Soviet journalists the opportunity to interview President Reagan, and the result, accompanied by a full-page rebuttal, appeared in *Izvestiia*. The 1985 Geneva Summit was given very wide coverage on Soviet television, and then came the simultaneous broadcasts of greetings by each country's leader on the television channels of the other on New Year's Day, 1986. The examples could be multiplied; all show that the range of what is permitted on the Soviet airways is much larger than in previous years and the issues are far more contentious.

It is undeniable that radical changes have been instituted in all components of the Soviet media. I noted earlier that television *created* the first mass public in Soviet history. I mean by this that the only significant experience this heterogeneous audience shares may, in fact, be media message. As George Gerbner has noted, "mass production and distribution of messages systems transforms selected private perspectives into broad public perspectives and brings mass publics into existence."[41] Television is the most credible medium in the United States, as Aleksandr Iakovlev no doubt observed during his stint in North America, and it is now also the most credible medium in the Soviet Union. Iakovlev has been quoted as saying "The TV image is everything."[42]

Western observers of the Soviet scene wonder about the motivation for the recent reforms. Are they intended to render more effective the manipulation or persuasion of the population (and thus buttress the regime more effectively) or are they a genuine opening of the system toward the recognition of public demands and needs and more plural inputs from that public? I would argue that the imposition of this dichotomy is not analytically helpful. As I have pointed out above, the dramatic new moves in media policy have a clear and stated intention to enhance the effectivess of that centralized and officially controlled system. It is thought that the changes will enable the system to do its job better—the job of informing and persuading the public. But the dilemma of the reforms is that, precisely in order to be more effective, the media must go some distance toward the satisfaction of public demand. If they do not, they will lack authority and credibility, and their mission will be preempted by other, nonofficial sources of information. Thus, the real question is not whether the public's assessment and preferences will play a role, but rather, how large a role that must be for the media to be as effective as theoretically and technologically they can be. Particularly with respect to television—the new electronic marvel spanning the country—these questions have become central.

But will this grandiose new plan to harness the media to dramatic, but not destabilizing, change work? There is considerable evidence of uncertainty and backlash: The limits of *glasnost'* are not yet clear. A *Pravda* correspondent has been reprimanded for inaccuracies in his exposé of economic mismanagement. An angry letter to *Izvestiia* was published castigating Phil Donahue for being a provocateur and saboteur, and Vladimir Pozner, the Soviet host of the televised space bridge, for unpatriotic behavior in sponsoring a show in which the expression of anti-Soviet views was allowed. In his day Nikita Khrushchev made radical changes without assessing their impact. Many of these changes—those in education, the arts, the military, and the role of the party in society—produced contradictory and, in some cases, dysfunctional results. They were called "hare-brained schemes." The television reforms of the Gorbachev period are derived from the same conviction, packaged, to be sure, in a much more modern way and tied to a seductive new technology. But the effects of these changes have not been seriously assessed by the Soviet leadership, and their contradictory and complex character has surely been underestimated.

Notes

1. *Narodnoe khoziaistvo* 1972, 314.
2. Fedotova, Kapeliush, and Sazonov 1985, 149.
3. Iushkiavichius 1985, 2.
4. For a good discussion of the development and deployment of Soviet comsats, see Campbell 1985.
5. Bagirov 1974, 102–103.
6. Iakovleva 1981, 60.
7. For a discussion of the education system of the Communist Party, see Mickiewicz 1967. For a discussion of the lecture system, see Mickiewicz 1981.
8. Telpugov 1979, 12.
9. Filippov and Slesarev 1981, 122.
10. Iushkiavichius 1985, 3.
11. Vakurova 1985, 19.
12. See Bagirov 1978.
13. Svitich and Shiriaeva 1979, 92.
14. *Sredstva massovoi informatsii* . . . 1984, 16, 36.
15. *Ibid.*, 36.
16. Rogers 1969, 770.
17. Khelemendik 1977, 117.
18. Bagirov 1978, 22.
19. Nozhin 1984, 31.
20. Abaiev 1985, 6.
21. Kishchik and Vostrukhov 1985, 3.
22. "Soviet Moves Against Videos . . ." 1986, 7.
23. Iushkiavichius 1985, 1.
24. Khelemendik 1977, 83.
25. Iushkiavichius 1983, 20–22.
26. Zadorkin and Sosnovskii 1977, 90–91.
27. Grushin and Onikov 1980. They also report that an hour of First Program (6:00–7:00 p.m.) is used for local broadcasts.
28. Fomicheva 1976, 106–13, 147.
29. Robinson and Levy 1986, 237.
30. These figures are based on a survey of news coverage in Hollander 1972, 43.
31. Shlapentokh 1970a, 61; and Shlapentokh 1970b, 172.
32. *"Literaturnaia Gazeta"* . . . 1978, 56.
33. Kelnik 1975, 137.
34. For a discussion of the new understanding of communication theory, see

Mickiewicz 1983.
  35. Zhavoronkov 1976, 60.
  36. Fomicheva 1976, 110–115, 132.
  37. Chekalova 1983, 3.
  38. Chernenko 1983. Gorbachev's formulation is in his keynote address to the 27th Party Congress in *Pravda*, February 26, 1986, p. 10.
  39. For differing views of this controversial episode at the Reykjavik summit in 1986, see William Safire, "You've Got a Deal!" in *The New York Times*, 10 November 1986, 21, and Letter from Charles Horner and John Korder (of the United States Information Agency), *The New York Times*, 20 November 1986, 28.
  40. For an excellent study of how such cognitive schemas work, see Graber 1984.
  41. Cited in Jowett and Linton 1980, 75.
  42. Salisbury 1986, 33.

Bibliography

Abaiev, K. 1985. "Pokazhet video." *Izvestiia*, 23 June, 6.

Bagirov, E. G. 1974. "Televidenie kak sotsial'nyi institut politicheskoi struktury obshchestva." In: *Zhurnalistika v politicheskoi strukture obshchestva*. Moscow.

————. 1978. *Ocherki teorii televideniia*. Moscow.

Campbell, Robert W. 1985. "Satellite Communications in the USSR." *Soviet Economy* (4) (October–December).

Chekalova, E. 1983. "Dialog u teleekrana." *Pravda*, 1 April.

Chernenko, Konstantin U. 1983. "Aktual'nye voprosy ideologicheskoi, massovopoliticheskoi raboty partii." *Pravda*, 15 June, 1–3.

Fedotova, L., Kapeliush, Ia., and Sazonov, V. 1985. "Televidenie v nebol'shom gorode." In: Sabashnikova 1985.

Filippov, F. P., and Slesarev, G. A., eds. 1981. *Formirovanie sotsial'noi odnorodnosti sotsialisticheskogo obshchestva*. Moscow.

Fomicheva, I. D. 1976. *Zhurnalistika i auditoriia*. Moscow.

Graber, Doris A. 1984. *Processing the News: How People Tame the Information Tide*. New York: Longman.

Grushin, B. A., and Onikov, L. A., eds. 1980. *Massovaia informatsiia v sovetskom promyshlennom gorode*. Moscow.

Hollander, Gayle Durham. 1972. *Soviet Political Indoctrination*. New York: Praeger.

Iakovleva, T. F. 1981. "Obespechenie vzaimosviazi khoziaistvennykh organizatsionnykh i vospitatel'nykh zadach v perspektivnykh planakh ideologicheskoi raboty." In: *Voprosy teorii metodov ideologicheskoi raboty*, vyp. 13. Moscow.

Iushkiavichius, G. 1983. "TV, rezervy tekhniki." *Zhurnalist* (1).

————. 1985. "Televidenie i radioveshchanie v novykh usloviakh." *Radio* (10).

Jowett, Garth, and Linton, James M. 1980. *Movies as Mass Communication*. Beverly Hills: Sage.

Kelnik, V. 1975. "Bolshoi mir i malenkaia gazeta (O vystupleniiakh na mezhdunarodnye temy v raionnoi i gorodskoi pechati)." In: *Gazeta i zhizn'*. Sverdlovsk.

Khelemendik, V. S. 1977. *Soiuz pera, mikrofona, i telekamery*. Moscow.

Kishchik, N., and Vostrukhov, E. 1985. "Videouroki." *Izvestiia*, 15 October.

"Literaturnaia Gazeta" i ee auditoria. 1978. Moscow.

Mickiewicz, Ellen. 1967. *Soviet Political Schools*. New Haven: Yale University Press.

————. 1981. *Media and the Russian Public*. New York: Praeger.

————. 1983. "Feedback, Surveys, and Soviet Communication Theory." *Journal of Communication* 33(2) (Spring), 97–110.

Narodnoe khoziaistvo SSSR, 1922–1972. 1972. Moscow.

Nozhin, Evgenii. 1984. "Ni slova ne vozmut na veru." *Molodoi Kommunist* (8) (August).

Robinson, John P. and Levy, Mark R. 1986. *The Main Source: Learning from Television News.* Beverly Hills: Sage.

Rogers, Rosemarie. 1969. "The Soviet Audience Expects and Gets More From its Media." *Journalism Quarterly* 46(4) (Winter).

Sabashnikova, E. S., ed. 1985. *Televidenie i zritel'.* Moscow.

Salisbury, Harrison. 1986. "Gorbachev's Dilemma." *The New York Times Magazine,* 27 July.

Shlapentokh, V. E. 1970a. "K voprosu ob izuchenii esteticheskikh vkusov chitatelia gazety." *Problemy sotsiologii pechati,* vol. 2. Novosibirsk.

———. 1970b. *Sotsiologiia dlia vsekh.* Moscow.

"Soviet Moves Against Videos Spreading 'Cult of Violence,'" *The New York Times,* 7 September 1986.

Sredstva massovoi informatsii i propagandy. 1984. Moscow.

Svitich, L. G., and Shiriaeva, A. A. 1979. *Zhurnalist i ego rabota.* Moscow.

Telpugov, Viktor. 1979. "Rasplachivaemsia zdorov'em." *Literaturnaia gazeta,* 15 August.

Vakurova, N. 1985. "Tele- i radioinformatsiia v zerkale obshchestvennogo mneniia." *Govorit i pokazyvaet Moskva,* 10 April.

Zadorkin, V. I., and Sosnovskii, A. V. 1977. "Perspektivy kommunikativnykh vozmozhnostei televideniia kak sredstva osveshcheniia kul'turnogo urovnia." In: *Issledovanie rosta kul'turnogo urovnia trudiashchikhsia.* Moscow.

Zhavoronkov, A. V. 1976. "Potreblenie materialov gorodskoi gazety." In: *Sotsiologicheskie problemy obshchestvennogo mneniia i deiatel'nosti sredstv massovoi informatsii.* Moscow.

AFTERWORD

Heyward Isham

The preceding essays have illuminated some of the dilemmas and tensions that Mikhail Gorbachev faces as he embarks upon a far-reaching, even revolutionary effort to "restructure" and revitalize Soviet economic and social life.

The Gorbachev program, approved at the June 1987 plenary session of the CPSU Central Committee, was derived from a consensus reached within the Soviet leadership after a fierce struggle between reformists and conservatives—a struggle that antedated Gorbachev's ascension in March 1985. Its premise is that the situation in the USSR had reached, in Gorbachev's phrase, the "pre-crisis" stage. Economic stagnation—reflected in declining rates of economic growth and labor productivity, and lagging technological and scientific adaptation—had reached the point that the USSR was falling behind the other Comecon countries (not to mention the Western industrial societies) in international competitiveness. It has been reported, for example, that only about 8 percent of Soviet machine tools can compete on the world market.

The situation in the workplace was bleak. As economist Nikolai Shmelev wrote in the June 1987 issue of *Novyi mir*, workers were succumbing to apathy, indifference, theft, contempt for hard work, and a fierce envy of those who earned good wages. Frustrated in their efforts to overcome social injustices, workers had become alienated from social goals. Many Soviet citizens, Shmelev continued, no longer believed that a better organization of economic and social life was even possible.

Ambassador Heyward Isham is a retired Foreign Service officer specializing in Soviet affairs.

Managers, too, had become disheartened, their careers spent battling a hypercentralized planning and pricing system that rewarded quantity, not quality, and discouraged competitiveness and innovation. Gorbachev put the issue succinctly in his report to the June 1987 plenum: "How can an economy make progress if it offers hot-house conditions for laggards, while hitting front-runners?"

The problem of consumer goods was another sore point. Despite shortages, those goods that were produced often went unsold, having been designed and manufactured with scant attention to consumer choice. Again in Gorbachev's words, "Work merely to stock warehouses is not only wasteful. It is absurd. . . . Better to close down such production."

The reform program takes on all of these problems; but few of the proposed solutions can be implemented without countervailing effects. Every policy choice involves the complex weighing of intractable elements—a situation that is exacerbated, it is now conceded, by the authoritarian, bureaucratic, and secretive style of many party, government, and economic officials. As Gorbachev insisted in his June 1987 plenum speech, the time of "orders, bans, and appeals" is past. And he acknowledged that the reform program would have to overcome ideological stereotypes that disparage as "alien to socialism" such things as competition, profitability, the role of market forces, greater autonomy for factory managers, and cooperative and individual ventures in the service industries.

It is clear that any process of renewal in the Soviet Union will require solutions that are seriously at odds with orthodox, neo-Stalinist notions of "socialism."

Consider the case of agriculture. There has been a wholesale abandonment of collective farms in the non–Black-Earth zones of central Russia, as the most energetic peasants have migrated to the towns and cities. Gorbachev has suggested that it would make sense to rent this land to whoever would like to farm it—an expedient that would dramatically expand the private sector in agriculture. In the case of industry, inefficient or poorly managed factories might be allowed to go bankrupt, and redundant workers could well lose their jobs. Certainly the price of bread and other commodities, subsidized to the tune of 73 billion rubles a year, will have to rise (although the authorities, recalling the Polish government's hard-learned lessons, are wary of precipitous action).

Both the myth of Soviet superiority, and the system of special privileges which many party functionaries have come to regard as inalienable rights, will undoubtedly suffer in the years ahead. Moreover, Soviet citizens can expect to find further shocking revelations of Stalin's crimes—and more sobering glimpses of unpleasant contemporary realities—in novels, memoirs, and poems, on the screen, stage, and television. Indeed, to many, the ideal of order—*poriadok*—appears to be under siege, and Gorbachev's proclaimed ideal of openness—*glasnost'*—seems tantamount to license. Yet others, particularly the young and the intellectuals, rejoice that a fresh wind is blowing at last.

Disaffected minority groups now dare to press their causes more insistently. Already, Crimean Tatars crusading to recover the ancestral lands from which they were expelled in 1944 have held a mass demonstration in Red Square. By the same token, Russian nationalist extremists—anti-Western, anti-Semitic, and surprisingly well organized—are pressing demands for police crackdowns on hippies and drug dealers. It is to be expected that they will continue to agitate (and in this they have broad support) for the preservation of cultural monuments and the protection of the environment.

Such ferment is inevitable, and necessary, if Soviet society is to be shaken from its torpor.

In his concluding remarks at the June 1987 plenum, Gorbachev defended his reform plan against unnamed opponents within the party apparatus, saying, "If somebody, fearing the complexities of the current stage, sits it out in his office in cowardly fashion, without reacting to the fact that life is knocking ever louder at the doors and windows, this will become the biggest mistake." Earlier, in a candid bid for the support of the Soviet scientific and literary establishment, he reportedly asked: "If not now, when? If not us, who?"

In his early novel *Julio Jurenito* (1922), Ilya Ehrenburg—whose 1954 novel *The Thaw* gave an unforgettably evocative name to Khrushchev's reform process—satirized the emerging postrevolutionary society. One of the characters, the Commissar, defends the need for continued coercion in these words: "We are driving [the people] forward, driving them to paradise with iron whips." Mikhail Gorbachev, no less a revolutionary than Ehrenburg's Commissar, knows that he must deal in different techniques, because the Soviet people (absent an attack on the homeland) have by now developed far too many forms of self-defense against state intrusion to tolerate coercion. His reform program has to be geared to a more cynical and better-educated Soviet society, one that has become more worldly-wise, self-absorbed, and materialistic.

As the essays in this volume suggest, the manner in which Gorbachev seeks to realize his vision, and the balance he is able to strike between ideology and social realities, between the party's monopoly of power and the practical necessity of broader and more spirited participation in the life of Soviet society, will determine whether his grand design succeeds or whether, like other efforts before his own, it withers away.

INDEX

Abortion, 12
Absenteeism, 35
Acmeist poetry circle, 102
Afghanistan, 106, 113, 146
Afonin, V., 103
Aganbegian, Abel, 96
Agriculture, 42, 84, 152
Aitmatov, Chinghiz, xii, 105, 106, 109, 114, 118, 120, 123
Akhmatova, Anna, 102, 188
Alcoholism, x, xi, 22, 31–32, 46, 52–75, 113, 123; antidrinking campaign, 52–75; black-market distribution of alcohol, 66; deaths from, 54; effect of price increases, 69; fiscal constraints, 61–62; home production, 65; poisoning, 66; publicity and propaganda, 56–60; results of antidrinking campaign, 62–69; state monopoly on alcohol, 61; traditional basis, 59; underground market for alcohol, 54–55; Voluntary Temperance Society, 57, 58, 60
Alekseev, Mikhail, 101
Alma-Ata, 19, 83, 88, 91, 98, 110, 145
Anan'ev, 115
Andropov, Iurii, vii, 32
Anti-Semitism, 60, 153
Armenia, 17, 83, 84, 85, 86, 90
Artsybashev, Mikhail, 106
Arutiunian, Iu. V. 77–78
Ashkhabad, 19, 83
Astaf'ev, Viktor, xii, 3, 104, 105, 112, 113, 114, 118, 123, 125

Azerbaijan, 67, 82, 83, 84, 85, 86, 90

Babaian, E. A., 58
BBC, 145
Bagirov, E. G., 133
Baikal-Amur Rail Line, 138–139
Baku, 19, 83
Balaian, Z., 58
Bashkiria, 26
Belorussia, 22, 24, 39, 82, 83, 84, 85, 86, 98; railroad experiment, 44–45
Birthrate, 24–25, 82
Blue-collar workers, 34–35, 39
Bolsheviks, 102, 126
Bondarev, Iurii, 124
Borovitskii Metro, 116
Brezhnev, Leonid, vii, 36, 39, 45, 46, 80, 89, 91, 94, 97, 98, 121
Bulgakov, Mikhail, 118
Bykov, Vasil', 118

Caucasus, 123, 124
Central Asia, 9, 13, 98, 116, 124
Cheliabinsk, 19
Cherkess, 95
Chernenko, Konstantin, vii, 39
Chernobyl, 144–145, 146
Child abuse, 123
Children of the Arbat, xii
Christianity, 105–106, 118
Communist Party, xiii; 42, 43, 95, 98, 101, 114, 118, 120, 139, 151, 152, 153
Comprehensive Program for Develop-

ment of Consumer Goods and Services Production in 1986–2000, 42

Crimean Tatars, 153

Culture, 101–115, 122; civic, 113; interpretation of problems, 107–120; signs of change, 101–106

Daghestan, 81

Dance, 111

Danilov, S., 124

The Day Lasts More Than One Hundred Years, 105

The Defense, 102

Divorce, ix, 18, 19, 21, 23, 63, 64, 115

Dnepropetrovsk, 19, 113

Doctor Zhivago, 101, 102

Donahue/Pozner space bridge, 146

Donetsk, 19

Don't Speed, Pal!, 103

Drugs. *See* Narcotics

Dry Inlet, 118

Dushanbe, 19, 83

"Dzhan," 123

Economic growth, 30–51, 151, 152

Education, 33, 85; applicants for higher school admission, 86; literary preferences, 93; ratio of higher school students to technicum students by nationality, 87; reading, 94, 108, 117; school reform, 39

Ehrenburg, Ilya, 153

El'tsin, Boris, 34, 116

Engels, Friedrich 9, 11

Erevan, 19, 83

Estonia, 83, 84, 85, 86, 87, 93

Evtushenko, Evgenii, 102, 106, 119

The Execution Block, xii, 105, 120, 123

Fadeev, Aleksandr, 117

Family, viii-ix, 3–29, 114–115; child abuse, 123; demographics in 1980s, 12–25; distribution, 14, 16; future, 25–27; illegitimate children, 22, 24; infant mortality, 23–24; modern, 7; policy, 9–12; preindustrial, 7; reasons for divorce, 23; marriages and divorces, 18, 19, 21; sociological conceptualization, 6–9

Fet, Afanasii, 109

The Fire, xii, 103, 112

Firestarter, 109

First Program, 139

Frunze, 19, 83

Furmanov, D., 117

Gamzatov, Ramzul, 124

Geneva Summit (1985), 146

Georgia, 67, 83, 84, 85, 86, 87, 90, 93, 125, 144

Gerbner, George, 147

Ginzburg, Lidia, 102

Glasnost', ix, 56, 60, 115–128, 142–148, 153

Glushkov, 62

Gogol', Nikolai, 102

Goncharov, Ivan, xiv

Gorbachev, Mikhail: antidrinking campaign, 52–75; biography, 95–97; discipline campaign, 32; economic objectives, 30–31; economic reform, 96–97, 152; labor policies, x, 45–46; and nationality problem, 98–99; policy initiatives and policy debate, 96–97, 151; political needs, 97–98, 153

Gor'kii, 19

Gorky, Maxim, 117

Gosteleradio, 134, 135, 138, 139

Granin, Daniel, 102

Gromyko, Andrei, 146

Grushin, B. A., 139

Gumilev, Nikolai, 102, 121, 122, 127

Gusev, S., 63

Health, 31–32, 54, 55

Iakovlev, Aleksandr, 145, 147

Industry, 42

Infant mortality, 23–24

Iskander, Fazil, 118

Islam, 81, 98, 118

Israel, 60

Iunost', 108

Iushkiavichius, G. K., 138, 139

Ivanova, Natalia, 108
Izvestiia, 140, 146, 147

Jaunsudrabin, J., 107
Jews, 86, 146; *see also* Anti-semitism
Julio Jurenito, 153

Kallistratov, Avdii, 105, 106
Kaltakhchian, Suren, 119
Karachai, 95
Karpov, V., 117, 118, 127
Kashtanov, A., 103
Kataev, Valentin, 118
Kaverin, Veniamin, 102
Kazakhstan, 65, 79, 80, 82, 83, 85, 86, 88, 98
Kazan', 19
KGB, 81
Khar'kov, 19
Khodasevich, Fedor, 102
Khrushchev, Nikita S., vii, 86, 102, 116, 147, 153
Kiev, 19
King, Stephen, 109
Kirghizia, 82, 83, 84, 85, 86, 88, 107
Kishinev, 19, 83
Kizhi, 116
Komsomol, 110, 138, 144
Komsomol'skaia pravda, 20, 119
Korean Airlines, 146
Korsunskii, L., 111
Kuibyshev, 19
Kunaev, Dinmukhamed 80, 98
Kunitsyn, Boris, 106, 124, 125
Kuznetsov, 117

Labor problems, 30–51; discipline, 40–41; excess supply of specialists, 32–35; Gorbachev's labor policies, 45–46; impact of alcohol on discipline and productivity, 54; labor force problems, 31–32, 151; lengthening the work week, 39; monetary rewards, 41–44; motivation, 40–45, 151; planning, 38; reconstruction, 37; renovation, 37; unearned incomes decree, 43–44; unemployment, 67, 152; worker shortages, 35–40; workplace reduction, 37, 152
Lake Baikal, 116
Lanshchikov, Anatolii, 116
Latvia, 83, 84, 85, 86
Latvian University, 107
Lenin, xii, 94, 96, 98, 111, 142
Lenin Library, 116
Leningrad, 19, 23, 113, 139
Leningrad experiment, 34
Leningrad regional committee, 38
Levins, Boris, 58
Levins, Mikhail, 58
Ligachev, Egor, 97
Likhachev, Dmitri, 103, 109, 119
Literaturnaia gazeta, 24, 107, 113, 116, 134, 140, 141
Lithuania, 83, 84, 85, 86
Lizichev, General, 96
Lysenko, Trofim, 58, 106

"Maiak," 135, 136
Malyshkin, A., 117
Mandelstam, Osip, 102, 107, 118
Marriage, 18, 19, 21
Marx, Karl, 9
Marxist doctrine, 142
Matevosian, Grant, 108
Media, viii, 9, 66, 67, 90, 98–99, 105, 115, 120, 122, 131–150; agenda-setting and international issues, 141–142; changes, 132–133; and *glasnost'*, 115, 116, 142–148; revolution, 137–138; social issues and media effectiveness, 138–141; Soviet policy, 146; television and radio, 107, 109, 116, 122, 133–136; videotape recorders, 136–138
Meilakh, Mikhail, 101
Meskhetian, 96
Ministry of Culture, 111
Ministry of Education, 144
Ministry of Finance, 62
Ministry of Health, 58
Ministry of Internal Affairs (MVD), 41, 56, 65
Ministry of Trade, 652

Minsk, 19, 83
Miroshnichenko, Nikolai, 107
Mishin, V., 110, 112
Mitterand, François, 146
Moldavia, 67, 85, 86, 90, 93
Moscow, 19, 34, 110, 116, 132, 137, 139, 140
"Moscow Does Not Believe in Tears," 138
Moscow University, 138
Moskva, 101
Muslim, ix, xi, 31, 82, 105

Nabokov, Vladimir, 101, 102, 121, 122, 123, 127
Nagibin, Iurii, 112, 123
Narcotics, 66, 113, 114, 115–116, 126, 153
Nationality, 76–100; applications for higher school admission, 86; changing size of Slavic and non-Slavic, 82; economic growth, 88–89; ethnicity, 78, Gorbachev's view, 98–99; indigenous population percentages, 83; literary preferences, 93; meaning, 76–94; migration, 83–84; nationalism, xi, 91, 92, 153; pay in agriculture, 84; ratio of higher school students to technicum students, 87; value orientations, 92; and years of schooling, 85
Nekrasov, Nikolai, 108
New York Daily News, 115
North Caucasus, 67
Novopolotsk system, 39, 40, 41
Novosibirsk, 19, 69
Novyi mir, 102, 151

Oblomov, xiv
Odessa, 19
Ogarkov, Marshal, 146
Oktiabr', 114
Omsk, 19
Onikov, L. A., 139
Orthodoxy, 118, 123, 127
Ossetian, 90
Ostrovskii, Nikolai, 117

Pasternak, Boris, 102, 118, 121
Paternity suits, 12
Pedlars, 103
Perevedentsev, Viktor, 13, 20, 23
Perm', 19, 22, 23
Petty Demon, 102
Pikul', Valentin, 109
Platonov, Andrei, 103, 123
Poem without a Hero, 102
Poet's Library, 102
Poland, 153
Population, ix, 25, 83
Pozner, Vladimir, 147
Pravda, 136, 140, 141, 144, 147
Pugacheva, Alla, 111

Rasputin, Valentin, xii, 103, 112, 113, 116, 123, 125
Reagan administration, 137–138, 146
Requiem, 102
Religion, 105–106, 118, 119
Riga, 19, 83, 137
Rostov, 139
RSFSR, 66, 83, 84, 86, 90
Ruble, Blair, x
Rumiantsev building, 116
Russian, 59, 79–80, 87, 95, 112, 122–127; language, 84–86, 122–125; nationalism, 96–97, 153
Rybakov, Anatolii, xii

The Sad Detective, xii, 3, 104, 105, 112
Sakhalin, 113
Sakharov, Andrei, 117, 146
The Sea of Youth, 103
Second Program, 139
Shchekino system, 34, 45
Shcherbitskii, Vladimir, 98
Shmelev, Nikolai 151
Sholokhov, Mikhail, 117
Siberia, 124, 132
Sidorov, Evgenii, 118
Silver Anniversary, 110
64, 101
Slavs, 123
Sobesednik, 111

Sobriety and Culture, 58, 60
Socialization, 4–5
Sologub, Fedor, 102
Solovetskii Island, 112
Solzhenitsyn, Aleksandr, 101, 117
Southern Tier, 9, 13, 15, 25
Sovetskii ekran, 110
Soviet Union: culture, 101–115, 122; divorce, ix, 18, 19, 21, 23, 63, 64, 115, 123; economic growth, 30–51; economy, ix, 30; family, xiii–ix, 3–29; family policy, 9–12; labor problems, 30–51; media policy, 146; nationality problem, 76–100; Russification, xii; socialization, 4–5; as an urban society, 12–13; women, 8; youth, 121–122
Stakhanov movement, 45, 117
Stalin, Iosif, vii, 11, 12, 13, 32, 76, 77, 89, 98, 102, 153
State Committee on Prices, 66
State Committee for Television and Radio Broadcasting, 139
Stavropol', 95
The Suit, 110
Sverdlovsk, 19

Taganka Theater, 110
Taganrog survey, 139
Tajikistan, 82, 83, 84, 85, 86
"Takyr," 123
Tallin, 19, 83
Tashkent, 19, 137
Tatars. *See* Crimean Tatars
Taxi Driver, 103
Tbilisi, 19, 83
Technology, 36
The Thaw, 153
Theater, 110–113
Three Sisters, 110
Tolstaia, Tat'iana, 108
Tolstoi, Aleksei, 117
Transcaucasian republics, 9
Tretiak, 111
Trud, 141
Tsirulis, G., 103
Tsvetaeva, Marina, 118

Turkmenistan, 83, 84, 85, 86
Tvardovskii, Aleksandr, 118
"12th Floor," 144

Ufa, 19
Uglov, Fedor, 58
Ukraine, 67, 82, 83, 84, 85, 86, 98, 113
Ul'ianovsk, 34, 64
Unemployment, 67
U.S. Department of State, viii
United States Information Agency, 145
Uzbekistan, 79, 82, 83, 84, 85, 86, 87, 90, 92, 93

Vilnius, 19, 83
Vlasov, A., 65
Voice of America, 145
Volgograd, 42
Voluntary Temperance Society, 57, 58, 60
Voprosy literatury, 102
Voronezh, 137
Voyage to the Islands, 112
Voznesenskii, Andrei, 102, 107
Vysotskii, Vladimir, 109

We, 102
White-collar workers, 33
Who Is Happy in Russia?, 108
Wick, Charles, 145
Women, 8; *see also* Family
World War II, 12, 13, 90
Writers' Congress, 102, 103, 116, 121, 124, 125
Writers' Union, 102, 105, 116, 117, 124, 127

Youth, 121–122

Zabotin, B., 65
Zalygin, Sergei, 102
Zamiatin, Evgenii, 102
Zhdanov, A. A., 127, 128
Zhdanovshchina, 101
Znamia, 103
"Znanie" Society, xiii, 133
Zvezda, 109